DIALOGUE
IS NOT
JUST TALK

Studies in the
Postmodern Theory of Education

Joe L. Kincheloe and Shirley R. Steinberg
General Editors

Vol. 289

PETER LANG
New York • Washington, D.C./Baltimore • Bern
Frankfurt am Main • Berlin • Brussels • Vienna • Oxford

Carolyn M. Shields
Mark M. Edwards

DIALOGUE
IS NOT
JUST TALK

A New Ground
for Educational Leadership

PETER LANG
New York • Washington, D.C./Baltimore • Bern
Frankfurt am Main • Berlin • Brussels • Vienna • Oxford

Library of Congress Cataloging-in-Publication Data

Shields, Carolyn M.
Dialogue is not just talk: a new ground for educational leadership /
Carolyn M. Shields, Mark M. Edwards.
p. cm. — (Counterpoints: studies in the postmodern theory of education; v. 289)
Includes bibliographical references and index.
1. Communication in education. 2. Educational leadership.
3. School improvement programs. 4. Postmodernism and education.
I. Edwards, Mark M. II. Title. III. Series: Counterpoints (New York, N.Y.); v. 289.
LB1033.5.S55   371.2'001—dc22   2004020880
ISBN 978-0-8204-7469-4
ISSN 1058-1634

Bibliographic information published by **Die Deutsche Nationalbibliothek**.
Die Deutsche Nationalbibliothek lists this publication in the "Deutsche
Nationalbibliografie"; detailed bibliographic data are available
on the Internet at http://dnb.d-nb.de/.

Cover design by Joni Holst

The paper in this book meets the guidelines for permanence and durability
of the Committee on Production Guidelines for Book Longevity
of the Council of Library Resources.

© 2005, 2015 Peter Lang Publishing, Inc., New York
29 Broadway, 18th floor, New York, NY 10006
www.peterlang.com

Printed in the United States of America

TABLE OF CONTENTS

FIGURES

INTRODUCTION

To listen to the news on any given day brings into stark awareness the difficulty of achieving understanding and peaceful co-existence. Indeed, talk of genocide in Africa, violent protests related to G8 and GATT summits, a world AIDS crisis, a roadmap to peace in the Middle East, prohibitions against travel by the World Health Organization—all remind us of the significant challenges faced by those who are concerned with the human condition.

Some (for example, Goodlad, 2001) argue that democratic education comprises our "last best hope" for achieving more peaceful and equitable conditions throughout the world. Yet, the United Nations' goal of achieving free universal primary education has been a moving target. First set at 1980 and then 2000, the year 2015 is the most recent, but already unattainable, target date (Colclough, 1993). Even in developed countries where free public education is a taken-for-granted benefit, there is widespread recognition that it is more successful serving middle-class children than those from minoritized groups. In the United States, for example, African-American, Hispanic, and American-Indian students are known to experience higher drop out rates, lower completion rates, and less school success than their Caucasian counterparts. In Canada, apart from First Nation students, poor school performance correlates more closely to lower socio-economic status than to ethnic or visible minority status. Recent accountability and standards movements highlight achievement gaps between various groups of students and prompt renewed calls for reform, equity, and social justice. The situation is no different in many other developed countries.

Our assumption is that if you, like us, are disturbed by some of the current global trends and the many educational responses that focus on deskilling of teachers, on conformity and uniformity of instruction and assessment, and on control of students rather than on communities of learners, you ache for something different. This book grows out of our deep conviction that we have stumbled upon a better, richer, fuller way of thinking about learning, leading, and living.

Rationale

Throughout the developed world, as school populations become more diverse, school leaders are deluged by demands for public accountability on high-stakes tests, for eradicating racism and bullying, and for promoting the social, emotional, and academic achievement of all students. The considerable diversity and complexity of school populations has also, in recent years, led to an increased acknowledgment of the failure of traditional rational, technical, scientific, and pseudo-scientific approaches to educational leadership that have proven inadequate to meet the needs of 21st century schooling.

Dominant approaches to educational leadership throughout the 20th century were strongly influenced by understandings of the world as viewed through the lens of Cartesian-Newtonian science, a worldview that tended to separate the intellectual domain and to elevate it over, material, social, emotional, or spiritual awareness. Understandings of leadership associated with such an emphasis on rationality focused on management techniques, including a division between those who thought and planned (Taylor, 1912; Fayol, 1916), and those who actually performed the work, and, hence, on managers finding ways to predict, order, and control workers. The "successful" educational leader was often seen as a charismatic, hierarchical but genial manager whose school was a safe, smooth, and efficient place of learning. Nevertheless, despite appearances, inequities and barriers to the participation and equitable attainment of marginalized groups could, and often did, remain hidden beneath the surface.

Despite the recognized failure of the rational and technical approaches to school leadership to promote equitable achievement for all students or to achieve reforms or restructuring that foster either social justice or deeply democratic schooling, "scientific" approaches to educational administration are alive and well. New books offering several easy steps for administrators and leaders, prescriptive approaches to management, and checklists for addressing complex challenges are still among current best-sellers— particularly among the more popular, "business-oriented" books on leadership. Recent attempts to define the knowledge base of educational administration (Hoy, 1994) or to achieve consensus about a "new center" for the field (Murphy, 1999) suggest that, for many people, the rational and technical perspective is still dominant. Nevertheless, the fierce debate that followed Murphy's proposed "school improvement" center for educational administration and the recent flurry of books and articles on educational leadership that reject the traditional rational, technical, functionalist, and prescriptive approaches raise the possibility that there may well be alternatives to these approaches to school leadership (see, for example, Beck & Murphy, 1994; Foster, 1986; Furman-Brown, 2002; Starratt, 1995).

In order to achieve the multiple purposes of schooling and to reconcile the competing political, social, cultural, and economic demands placed on educators, more and more people are becoming interested in the moral purposes of leadership, in ethical leadership (Sergiovanni, 1992), and in the potential of dialogue as a focus for teaching and leadership (Burbules, 1993; Edwards & Shields, 2002).

Bryck (1988) reminds us the emphasis on dialogue is not new, but that:

> In writings as ancient as Aristotle, as contemporary as Gadamer, Habermas, and Arendt, as secular as Dewey, and as religious as Aquinas, we find strong support for the contention that the survival of a pluralistic democracy requires a belief that mutual understanding among diverse parties can be achieved through genuine dialogue and commitment of its citizens to such discourse. (p. 259)

Purpose

The purpose of this book is to explore how educational leaders may better comprehend and use dialogue to develop new educative relationships and to deepen understanding, which, in turn, may lay the groundwork for changing schools in ways that will enhance social justice and promote educational excellence. We argue that current approaches to educational leadership have not succeeded in this task. As educators, we have failed to create schools that are just, excellent, inclusive, and deeply democratic.

We will demonstrate in this book that dialogue, if understood as a powerful and creative force may, offer a meaningful way forward. We will show how conceptualizing dialogue as multifaceted—constituted by understanding and relationship, as ontologically universal and as epistemologically significant—can provide both an anchor and focus for a new approach to educational leadership.

For us, dialogue is not just another word for "talk," but a way of being in relation to other, often different, ideas, cultures, perspectives, and, yes, people. It is a complex and powerful dynamic, one that whirls and spirals and evolves—one that is central to our emotional, social, and cognitive being, but that may begin with the simplest of human interactions.

Challenges, Assumptions, and Caveats

Rather than elaborate a complex definition of dialogue at this point, and cognizant of the risk of provoking our readers' ire, the foregoing will have to suffice for now. We do not think it helpful to begin with a definition of dialogue beyond what we have indicated—a dynamic force that holds us in relation to others and deepens understanding. Speaking of dialogue in the necessarily linear sentences, paragraphs, pages, and chapters of a book is both difficult and frustrating, as the ideas and concepts interact, build, evolve, and interact again. Thus, you will find in this book some ideas that are repeated with new nuances and iterations and others that are introduced in each succeeding chapter as we delve deeper into the topic.

When we first became excited about the potential of dialogue as a basis for thinking and acting differently, for a more just and excellent educational praxis, we looked for a book that would help us. Having approached several publishers in our quest, we were finally urged to write the book that we sought in anticipation that others will find it useful as well. The thoughts and reflections you will find here are those that we, as educators committed to social justice and academic excellence, have found to be useful. We do not claim to be philosophers or historians or sociologists, although we have some knowledge of these disciplines. We do not attempt to represent thoroughly or precisely any individual positions or theoretical perspectives about ontology, epistemology, philosophy, history, or sociology; instead we have taken ideas that seem to us to hold promise for new approaches to school leadership and tried to construct a tower from which a new horizon of possibilities may be glimpsed, a parapet on which others may both stand and continue to build.

We write as one, yet we come to the task with very different lived experiences, academic backgrounds, and insights. We have spent hours talking about the ideas in this book, becoming more and more energized by them and increasingly convinced of their value. We have found that by writing a book about dialogue, we have engaged in dialogue and, in so doing, increased our understanding of the topic and deepened our relationship with each other. The process itself has been challenging, exciting, and powerful— one that has persuaded us that we are "on to" something.

Sometimes the task has presented challenges, as when we wanted to share an incident or episode that one of us experienced. Sometimes we write "I" without trying to clarify whether the story you are reading originated with Mark or with Carolyn, for the power is in the narrative and not the "ownership." For the most part, we simply write "we," accepting it as the best way we know to characterize the dialogical process.

Sometimes the problem that presented itself was which form of a word to use. For example, except where we are citing someone else's work, we have settled on *empathic* rather than *empathetic* (a later form of the same word). More difficult were decisions about two key concepts in the book. The use of the nouns *dialogue* and *carnival* is easy, but when it comes to their adjectival forms, we debated, waivered, engaged in the to-and-fro of dialogue, and finally came down on the side of the ambiguous "both-and." We have found that sometimes the word *dialogic* seems to work best; at other times, *dialogical* seems to have a more rhythmic sound in a given context. Hence, we use the two words interchangeably. Likewise, when we set out, we used the term *carnivalesque* as the adjective best suited to one aspect of dialogue. Then, in one translation of Bakhtin's work, the translator used *carnivalistic*. Again, we decided to use both terms, depending on what we believed best fit the poetry of the situation. We hope that the use of multiple terms provides you with additional ways of expressing these important concepts and that it enriches, rather than confuses, our presentation.

Our knowledge of the original sources that have inspired us has deepened and our respect for some of the thinkers who have preceded us— Bakhtin, Buber, Einstein, Freire, Gadamer, and others—has heightened. But we are also aware that these male writers, themselves situated in a different temporal context, have relied almost exclusively on male nouns and pronouns to express their ideas. Today, their words are sometimes jarring because of this, yet those who have known these scholars insist that their use of gendered terms comes from the traditions of their age in which certain "male" pronouns were assumed to be inclusive. Where we comment on or extend their ideas, we have tried to be sensitive to the language we use, selecting both male and female adjectives and pronouns alternately to express our thoughts. Where we cite from any of these authors, we have not changed their language. And it is our hope that the historically situated, legitimate concerns of our age around their obviously gendered use of language will not impede engagement with their powerful ideas.

Overview

We have wrestled with the limitations of presenting what are inextricably linked ideas in the linear format necessitated by a book. At times, we have somewhat arbitrarily decided that certain ideas belong in one chapter rather than another; at other times, we have introduced an idea at one point and signalled its further development elsewhere.

The book is divided into two sections. The introduction to Part One provides an overview of what we mean by dialogue and shows why we believe it offers a way forward for school leaders. We conceptualize dialogue as a creative and sustaining force that permits us to overcome the excessive instrumentality and bureaucracy of today's schools. In Chapter One, we demonstrate how current thinking about leading organizations has resulted in the dominance of instrumental thinking, an emphasis on technical strategies, and the imposition of prescriptive approaches to leadership. In this chapter, we demonstrate how the need for dialogue has been created over the centuries, as various theories and forces have emphasized thinking about educational organizations and their leadership in terms of management and efficiency. We also demonstrate the necessity of developing a new and original approach to leadership and the futility of continued tinkering with existing approaches. We believe that this brief romp through history provides the basis for understanding why dialogue offers more promise than existing approaches. If you are already familiar with the historical development of the field of educational leadership, you may want to skim or even skip this chapter and dive directly into Chapters Two and Three.

These chapters develop the two ideas that we present as foundational to understanding dialogic leadership and demonstrate clearly why we believe so strongly in its power. Chapter Two takes on the concept of relations and relationships, while Chapter Three takes up the intertwining theme of understanding—both aspects of being—that dialogue fosters, enables, and enhances.

Having explored the fundamental concepts related to our investigation of dialogue, we turn, in Part Two, to reflection on how dialogue may help educational leaders to foster deeply respectful and inclusive school communities in which people come together, acknowledging the intrinsic worth of each member of the community, in playful, creative, and empowering interactions. Thus, Chapter Four introduces some criteria for assessing whether school communities are socially just and academically excellent and whether they use power wisely and appropriately or in negative and oppressive ways. Chapter Five presents an image of dialogue as fundamental to community living, while Chapter Six extends this exploration by delving more deeply into alternative, boundary-breaking ways to overcome some of the hierarchical and organizational barriers to living together in deeply democratic communities.

The conclusion weaves together the threads of the other sections, focusing on the creative, empowering, and liberating aspects of dialogue and generating a rich, new approach both for educational leaders and the communities of which they are a part. It is our hope that as we reflect together on new ways to think about school leadership, we will come closer to images of schools as places of learning that nourish, rather than stifle, the full development of the children and adults who live so much of their lives in them.

Acknowledgments

Our lives are full of relationships that have blessed us with support and deepened our understandings and commitments. We cannot hope to thank or acknowledge here all of the family and friends, educators, other colleagues, and students who have influenced us on this journey. We do, however, want to particularly thank our children, who have consistently taught us that there is more than one way to look at the world; Carolyn's father and brother, who have flattered her with their reading of, and comments about, her previous work and who have, as always, been interested in and supportive of this present venture; Mark's father and mother, whose passion for understanding and dialogical relationship have permitted Mark a lifetime of shared openness and cherished dialogues with them and with his siblings; Cathy, with whom dialogue happens most deeply for Mark and with whom a lifetime will be too short.

We acknowledge our colleagues in the Department of Educational Studies at UBC and especially members of our research group, as many of them have spent long hours engaging with us in dialogue about dialogue. We also recognize with gratitude those whose contemporary work on dialogue and education has inspired us, especially Nicholas Burbules and Alexander Sidorkin, with whom we have established relationships that have encouraged us in this endeavor. We would be remiss if we did not acknowledge the support and encouragement of Joe Kincheloe and Shirley Steinberg, who were convinced that we could write something others would find helpful. We hope this book fulfills their belief in us.

Concluding Comment

Our opening and inviting concept of dialogue as a ground for educational leadership is that which enables the leader to enter into relationship with another and to develop understanding across whatever differences may exist (role, ethnicity, ability, level of education, gender, age, religious orientation, first language, and so forth). We believe that if we, as moral individuals and as educators, come to a better understanding of dialogue, open ourselves to it, and commit ourselves to it, we will indeed, as Bryck (1988) suggested in the elegant passage cited earlier, help to achieve both the survival and the promise of a pluralistic democracy.

It is our hope that this book will assist educational leaders to reflect on the nature of their organizations, the people who inhabit them, the relationships that exist and might exist, and the ways in which dialogue may help them to create more inclusive, respectful, just, and optimistic forms of schooling. By engaging in this conversation, we will, together, become more aware of the potential to re-create ourselves and our educational institutions.

Our thinking about dialogue, offered in this book, is simply a beginning. Our own understandings of dialogue are constantly being modified as we engage with one another, talking together about what we believe is important to write. For you, its meaning will likely also change, and hopefully deepen, as you engage with us in various aspects of dialogue in the next few chapters. We are cognizant that you will find in our text your own meanings, meanings that will continue to evolve as you read and reflect. We hope that the journey will be as profitable for you as it has proven to be for us.

PART ONE

Dialogue as Promise

*"Hopeless High School" is a medium-size, multiethnic school located in a mixed, but relatively low socio-economic area of a large urban center. By reputation, the school is a difficult, challenging, and overwhelming place to work. Teachers posted there receive expressions of sympathy from their peers: "Oh, I'm so sorry you are being sent to **that** school!" Students often seem to be going through the motions. Although they show up for class, more often than not, their homework is not done; they make little eye contact, sitting instead with ball caps shading their faces and responding, when asked, in monosyllables. Parents are rarely seen in the school, except when forced to come to the office to discuss some disciplinary action related to their child.*

Teachers and school administrators are at their wits' end. They have tried new curricula, computerized math programs, and anti-racist and anti-bullying programs and have created elaborate new discipline and attendance policies. Afterschool tutoring is in place; classes to teach students how to write tests, how to take notes, and how to study have been introduced. Yet nothing seems to have made a difference. The school is still labeled "low performing," and jobs and resources are on the line.

When educators are asked to clarify the problems, some familiar themes emerge. Parents are busy, too tired, too poor, or too disconnected from the school to help. Students come from dysfunctional families for whom formal education is not important. Teachers cannot be expected to be social workers, community workers, and health-care workers as well as teachers.

***

This depiction of a medium-sized urban high school is a composite of factual elements and experiences taken from several schools. In some ways, it is therefore more myth than fact; yet it is recognizable in that it contains attitudes and practices that are common in many schools in many developed countries. Hopeless High School is, in fact, the "shadow side" of Any High School—it highlights the elements that come into play when relationships break down, when progress toward identified goals seems painfully absent, or when test scores become the sole measure of student achievement. Many educators, students, and parents experience moments of intense disenchantment with schooling that seems to be increasingly high pressured,

but irrelevant and superficial. At such times, they may resonate deeply with
the negativity of the opening vignette. There is little in Hopeless High to
evoke a vibrant, happy, or exciting place of living and learning.

In Chapter One, we present an overview of some old but still influential
and pervasive ways of thinking about schools and educational leadership that
constrain our ability to move beyond Hopeless High School. And yet, we
believe that educators can create schools that are pulsating, exciting, caring,
and successful. We have become convinced that if one carefully examines
those elements of a school that are represented by Hopeless High School, one
will find relatively superficial interactions between and among educators and
the students. We also know that there are moments of caring and connection
in which some students are engaged and successful. One may find little
evidence of explicitly respectful or inclusive practices, supportive policies, or
joyful interactions. Nevertheless, on occasion, one may stumble across
evidence of participation and respect. The principal may know little of the
daily lives of either teachers or students, their responsibilities, their struggles,
or their successes, for she is often consumed with keeping the school running
and meeting all of the fiscal and achievement accountability mandates
imposed by law. The perspective of students is rarely sought, and the voices
of parents are duly silenced by teachers who believe that parents from this
neighborhood have little to offer even if they could convince them to come to
the school for a meeting. Yet we also identify occasions when teachers and
parents have worked together on a common project and developed new
respect and insight about the other's situation.

Unfortunately, as many school communities go through the motions of
their daily routines, Hopeless High is ever present in some form. There are
too few spaces, either physical or psychological, in which meaningful
relationships can be built and people can come to enjoy being and learning
together.

Paradoxically, the dominant social relations in many schools are those of
conflict and stress. Referrals to the vice-principal for disciplinary action are
so frequent that students may feel that their case is futile. It is hard to get a
hearing to communicate with an angry teacher one's deep desire to study, do
well, and graduate from high school. It is difficult to share one's feelings of
shame when the power has been cut off and there is no electricity at home
because a parent has failed to pay the bill. Doing homework in the dark is
really not an option. But understanding is. We can choose to develop
relationships and understanding that have the potential to make schools

joyful and optimistic learning communities. And we believe that dialogue is the key.

Achaan Po, a Thai Buddhist monk and one of Mark's mentors and teachers, once said: "We all have experience with what enlightenment is." Although we may not have called it *enlightenment*, we all have some fleeting memories of moments of deep insight, of absolute, unconditioned awareness. We are convinced that, in like fashion, although we may not have recognized them, each of us also has experience with what dialogue is—with moments of intense and satisfying connection with another human being when we have felt reciprocal and remarkable openness, moments that were both deeply affirming and highly exhilarating. For some of us, these moments occurred in the intimacy of a loving family, with a partner, a child, or a sibling with whom we felt totally accepted and deeply loved. Others, like Mark and Carolyn, have been fortunate enough to experience additional dialogical relations with friends with whom one has spent hours discussing, debating, and exploring some of the deepest mysteries of life.

We believe that these cherished moments reflect the ontological nature of dialogue; each holds in itself a constellation of ideas that promises new ways of being, relating, and understanding for leaders. The richness of dialogue, at an unconscious level, is part of our inheritance, part of what makes our lives vibrant and meaningful. But we are also convinced that it is essential to bring to a level of explicit awareness the potential of dialogue to create and sustain ever-deepening relationships and understanding. In this conviction lies what we believe is new and important and innovative about this approach to educational leadership and its potential to help transform our schools and our society.

We argue that if the principal and teachers of Hopeless High School were to focus on developing more positive relationships with each other and with their students and their parents, deeper levels of understanding would occur, understanding that could form the basis for more engaging, more relevant, and more optimistic educational opportunities. In other words, we are arguing that they need to engage in dialogue to help them make sense, both cognitively and experientially, of the world in which they live and work.

Understanding Dialogue: A Beginning

When we approach the topic of dialogue, we naturally begin with some assumptions. Not all talk is dialogue; neither is all dialogue talk. Dialogue is intricately complex but profoundly simple. It generally involves more than one person, although at times one can have profound internal dialogue; it generally involves the use of words, but there are languages of aesthetics, emotion, and human connection that do not always require words. Dialogue is not therapy: it does not require "telling all," although it does require engagement *with* another person or persons. To engage in dialogue one needs a modicum of trust and some degree of relationship with another person, although paradoxically, dialogue grows out of, and aids in, the development of both trust and relationships. Dialogue cannot happen if one treats another person as an "object," but only as one engages the other with what we are calling "absolute regard"[1] (Starratt, 1991), with respect for his or her intrinsic worth as a human being. Absolute regard is a phrase we use frequently. Used by Starratt to describe a quality of leadership in school communities, the phrase captures the essence of the ethical imperative that is fundamental to dialogue as understood by many of the authors on whose work we draw.

Dialogue, as a word, has a long history. In particular, it comprises two main ideas: *dia*, which means *across* or *through*, and *logos*, *word*. The etymology is important, for we often think of dialogue as a conversation or interaction between two people, misinterpreting the prefix *dia* for "di" (meaning two). Likewise, *logos* does not simply mean "word" in the sense of an utterance or text, but rather has rich and evocative connotations. Often associated with religious concepts found in the Bible, such as the creative word, the spirit, or the breath of life, the term was widely used in Hellenistic Greece and even earlier by pre-Socratic Greek philosophers. Heraclitus, for example, a Greek philosopher of the late 6th century B.C., used the term to signify an ordering principle of the world. For him, *logos* represented the unity that exists in experience, the oneness in which all things participate in some sense (see *Heraclitus*). This is consistent with *Webster's Dictionary of the English Language*, in which *logos* is defined as "reason, regarded as the controlling principle of the universe." The implication of reason, thought,

---

[1]   The term comes from J. R. Starratt, who used it in connection with building an ethical school. Although our purpose is slightly different, the term is critical to our concept of dialogue for educational leaders.

understanding is hence contained within the term *logos*, the creative word.[2]

At different periods over the centuries, philosophers and scholars have been attracted by the rich lineage and complex associations related to the concept of dialogue. We have been inspired and enlightened by many of them. We look, for example, to the insights of Martin Buber, whose articulation of the now well-known distinction between "I-it" and "I-Thou" relationships is central to our thinking. Freire and Noddings have, like us, been influenced by Buber and their ideas have informed our own: Freire's concept of *conscientization* and Noddings' concern with *care* are essential to our views on dialogue and dialogic leadership. Hans-Georg Gadamer, the 20th-century German philosopher at the center of hermeneutic thought, characterizes dialogue as a "to-and-fro movement," a sort of "play" among participants who bring to the activity a committed openness to the other. He describes new understandings metaphorically with reference to the expansion of participants' horizons. The 20th century Russian literary critic Mikhail Bakhtin notes that dialogue is a way of standing outside something, apart from someone, but seeking to understand: "It is immensely important for the person who understands to be *located outside* the object of his or her creative understanding—in time, in space, in culture" (1986b, p. 7). Thus, dialogue is a way for us to understand something or someone who is in some way different from ourselves, who has a different perspective, alternative lens, varied history, and so forth.

Our purpose here is not to present a bibliography of those whose work we cite throughout this book, but rather to remind the reader that scholarship about dialogue is not new, and that it is complex and important. Others have engaged in much more thorough and comprehensive analyses and discussion than we have opportunity to develop here. In fact, our purpose is slightly different. Rather than explore dialogue for its own sake, although that is an important and difficult task, we aspire to develop a concept of dialogue that will be robust enough for others to stand on, one that will prove accessible and useful to educators and educational leaders. In this vein, the insights of two other more contemporary scholars who have also taken up the concept of dialogue, Burbules (1993) and Sidorkin (1999, 2002), have helped to clarify our thinking and move this work forward.

---

[2] It is this connotation of reason, *explanation*, or a way of thinking and making meaning that *logos* as a suffix (-ology) also brings to disciplinary thinking, as in psychology, sociology, anthropology, and so forth.

Our understanding of dialogue is relatively eclectic in that we have drawn ideas from others where they seem to fit together into a meaningful and useful whole. It is practical in that our goal is to help educators reflect on new ways of being, both as human beings and as educational leaders; and it is deeply ethical, grounded in the need for absolute regard for the other.

Moving Forward

Our concept of dialogue is therefore organic, multifaceted, and dynamic. It is difficult, if not impossible, to define in one or two sentences. Moreover, when we use the noun *dialogue*, it suggests a fixed and static existence, rather than fluidity and perpetual transformation. We hesitate to suggest using dialogue as a verb, as that may confine it to the status of an instrumental process or strategy. Nevertheless, because a verb in some ways describes a process that is both active and creative, there are elements of a verb in our concept of dialogue. It is both verb and noun, a dynamic and an act, a way of interacting and the interaction itself, a way of understanding and the significance itself, a way of relating and the relationship itself.

Our challenge is to suggest a force that has the power and creative force implied by the Greek use of the word *logos,* a word that represents the creative life force of the universe. We do not use *dialogue* to imply a simple conversation (although a conversation may indeed be dialogic in the deeper meaning of the term).

In the next three chapters, we present some basic concepts related to dialogue. In Chapter One, as we have said, we examine how and why current approaches to educational leadership may have reached the limits of their potential to reform and transform the educational experiences of children. In Chapters Two and Three, we develop two fundamental entry points into dialogue. The first point of entry (Chapter Two) is the primacy of relationships. Here, we demonstrate how dialogue can create and sustain meaningful relationships, helping us change the ways in which we relate to and come to care for other people. Chapter Three takes a different approach and uses cognition as its entry point to show that dialogue may also change the ways in which we develop understanding and come to know one another.

Yet, even as we write these words, we are aware that as relationships change, so too does understanding, and that as understanding deepens, relationships change. The process is both spiral and not spiral as the forms themselves are altered, as they whirl in a myriad of indeterminate and unanticipated ways. Cognizant of the limitations of a static figure, after considerable to-and-fro and back-and-forth, we present Figure 1 as a graphic organizer and visual heuristic.

Figure 1. Three Dimensions of Dialogue

While it in no way captures the dynamic and creative qualities of dialogue, the figure graphically portrays the three primary dimensions we argue are essential to dialogue. It also reminds us that even as these dimensions are essential to dialogue, dialogue is central to being, to relationships, and to understanding. As we indicated earlier, the second section of the book will build on individual dialogical interactions and focus on the communal aspects of dialogue.

CHAPTER ONE

Objects and Objectivity

Principal Strong: Well, Mrs. Davis, your son, David, has been caught fighting and so, according to our rules, we will have to suspend him for three days. As you know we have a zero- tolerance policy for fighting.

Mother: I know those are the rules, but his dad had just left us, David was upset, and then one of his classmates called him a name.

Principal Strong: I'm sorry to hear that, but it really does not have anything to do with this situation. David knows that we do not condone fighting at this school, so I have no choice. He can return to school next Wednesday after he apologizes to Michael and to his teacher.

***

The above exchange rings true for anyone who has spent much time in a school office; indeed, it is repeated countless times a day in schools across the country. How do we get to the point in schools where we feel we have no choices, where finding alternatives to "rules" makes us appear to be weak or ineffective leaders? How do we get to the point where the disintegration of a family is less important than following the rules? And is there anything that educational leaders might do differently?

For approximately 60 years, scholars and practitioners have asked questions about what type of person is best fitted to be an educational leader.

Are there specific characteristics, traits, or leadership styles that one needs, or can learn, to enable one to be a better leader? While the outcomes of most of the studies about characteristics, traits, and strategies have been inconclusive, indicating, at best, that different skills are needed by different people in different situations, there is still a persistent quest for how to make educational leadership more effective or more successful. Even as we write the words "effective" and "successful," we are cognizant of the fact that many theorists are concerned about narrow, technicist conceptions of *effectiveness* that reflect a harsh, economic bottom-line, profit-making version of efficiency. Many practitioners are consumed by the need to focus on the increasingly high-stakes accountability movements that are occurring in education throughout much of the developed world, movements that seem to equate *success* with higher scores on norm-referenced, standardized tests.

We, educators and the general public alike, are also preoccupied with educational reform, improvement, restructuring, and the like; we are concerned about the achievement gaps between more affluent and impoverished students; we are anxious about reports of racism, bullying, violence, and increased dropout rates among members of minoritized groups; and we are determined to create schools that will promote respect, inclusion, and democratic citizenship.

In part because of rapid demographic changes, transformations in social and cultural norms, and increased pressure for public accountability, educators are also well aware of the rapidity with which policy, programs, and conceptions of "best practice" are revised and change is thrust upon us. Indeed, among educators, resistance is frequently conceptualized as closing one's classroom door and waiting out the newest "fad."

What is fascinating is to realize how old these problems are. A brief overview of centuries of thinking about how to find appropriate and valid standards for living, for knowing the "good" or "discovering the truth," provides insight into how we have come to the current state of knowledge and practice of educational leadership and why we firmly believe we need different and better ways of addressing the challenges and opportunities that confront leaders today.

The following sprint through time will demonstrate clearly how a philosophy or approach that was once intended as a corrective to a perceived imbalance can itself become the new orthodoxy, distorting and over-emphasizing the very "wrong" it was perceived to "right." One wonders if we will ever learn the lesson, if we will ever be able to find the appropriate balance in our attempts to be educational leaders, if we will ever be able to recognize some of the ideologies that continue to bias and influence our thinking.

A cynic might well ask whether this current examination of *dialogue* is simply another fad, another sign of the pendulum swinging in educational theory. We believe it is not, although you will have to judge for yourselves. We are convinced that there are so many demands already placed on educators that it is no longer possible to continue adding to what is already an overloaded agenda. Our dialogical approach is, therefore, not an add-on, but a new ground for leadership, one that starts with the need to create situations in which relationships and understanding are fundamental to action.

Educational Administration: Early Days

The 17th century was a time of great scientific and intellectual advances that laid the groundwork for much current thinking, a time in which great thinkers sought to better understand the world in which they lived and to determine some of its eternal truths. Today, we not only acknowledge our debt to the past, and its legacy to us, but decry some of its excesses, particularly those of rationality and mechanical or technical thinking. The influential history of this century is oft repeated and fills many library shelves. Descartes began his first *Meditation* with these words:

> Some years ago I was struck by a large number of falsehoods that I had accepted as true in my childhood, and by the highly doubtful nature of the whole edifice that I had subsequently based on them. I realized that it was necessary, once in the course of my life, to demolish everything completely and start again right from the foundations if I wanted to establish anything at all in the sciences that was stable and likely to last. (in Garber, 1998, p. 125)

His famous "Cogito" argument—"I think, therefore I am"—constituted his starting point for an indubitable truth. Impressed with the ability of mathematicians to demonstrate "truth," he determined to employ a similar "scientific" method in his own intellectual endeavors and thus developed a set of theorems and laws as predictable and immutable as mathematical formulas. Descartes' focus on the clarity of rational thinking led him to differentiate the thinking soul (subject) from the material world (object).

Although Descartes' philosophy was extremely influential in the 17th century, he was not the only one to move rational approaches in new directions. Among other important scientists such as Copernicus, Brahe, and Galileo, two stand out as having made especially significant contributions to modernist thinking. Bacon (1620) sought knowledge that would be based on empirical observation and experimentation and that would be practical and useful to human existence. The new direction was sealed when Isaac Newton, who in his later life devoted his time to writing on theology, joined Descartes' quest for rational truth and Bacon's sense of the importance of empiricism and, based upon careful observation of objects, developed his laws of mechanics. Often paired with Descartes in the term "Cartesian-Newtonian science," Newton's understanding of the world as a "thing" that responded mechanically to a set of fixed mathematical laws made a significant and lasting mark on the thinking of the Western world. Indeed, with the emphasis on a mechanistic "clockwork" view of the cosmos, science was firmly established not only as "a" way of knowing, but as "the" way of knowing.

Taken together, Descartes, Bacon, and Newton form a triumvirate symbolizing reason's optimistic and modern roots, roots from which new knowledge sprouted in every aspect of human endeavor. Subsequently, Adam Smith (1776/1996) applied these conceptual roots to modes of production, and efficiency as economic rationality became a new goal. The Industrial Revolution transformed the entire structure of society around new technologies, including rationalizing governing power structures into bureaucracies capable of "managing" large numbers of people. The natural world was adapted to suit human needs and desires at an exponential rate. Technological advances in weaponry permitted the development of massive, highly structured armies that colonized the world, wreaking havoc, killing millions, and reaching its logical conclusion in the grotesque "rationality" of the "Final Solution," the atomic bomb, and other so-called weapons of mass destruction.

Early in the 21st century, we are aware of the devastating excesses of much of what was once considered "progress"; yet, we cannot escape the pervasive influence of bureaucratic and mechanistic thinking and the adulation of rationality. Descartes, Bacon, and Newton provided us with new and powerful ways to engage the world, but relying too heavily on their approaches has led us to the brink of destruction.

Their influence has been no less pervasive, often with dehumanizing effects, in educational practice and theories of educational leadership. We have yet to determine appropriate limits to rational, mechanical, and bureaucratic theories of life in organizations or in human communities. Despite their still pervasive use in current practice, we recognize the failure of these approaches to help us deal with challenges such as the one posed by Mrs. Davis and her son David. The opening vignette exemplifies the need for educators and educational leaders to exercise discernment and to move beyond the thinking of the 17th century as a basis for 21st century praxis and moral action; it demonstrates how, too often, we treat individuals more as things belonging to the material world than as individuals with whom relationships and individualized interactions are necessary.

The Instrumentality of Education

The foregoing cursory examination of some of the early development of scientific thinking and the establishment of scientific, intellectual, and rational approaches to knowing provides the backdrop for our examination of the development of schooling in North America as well as of educational administration as an extension of scientific management.

Organizations (the word comes from the Greek *organon,* meaning "tool or instrument" [see Morgan, 1997, p. 15] and reminiscent of Bacon's *The New Organon*) are generally created to fulfill a specific need or purpose in society. Given the origins of the word and the highly bureaucratic concepts that undergird most organizational structures, the emphasis on instrumentality can be easily understood.

Public schooling in North America originated before the establishment of compulsory, free, public education in both the U.S. and Canada in the early 19th century.[1] Nevertheless, the compulsory school movement provides a useful starting point for an examination of schools as bureaucratic and instrumental institutions. Tyack (1974) describes how, in 1852, even before the compulsory education law of Boston, Massachusetts, schools had become institutions for socializing, sorting, and often segregating various social groups in society. Along with a strong police force, public education was seen as a means of maintaining social order and "stringent legislation [was passed] to force truants to go to school" and remove them from the decadent influence of "the streets" (Tyak, p. 68). Tyak continues, "The school

---

[1]   Horace Mann in Massachusetts and Edgerton Ryerson in Canada are generally considered the "fathers" of compulsory public schooling in their respective countries.

committee had created de facto segregation by establishing intermediate schools catering to poor and immigrant children" (p. 69). Tyak cites the state superintendent in California who, in the 1880s, wrote that "citizens should support compulsory education to save themselves from the rapidly increasing herd of non-producers ... to save themselves from the wretches who prey upon society like wild beasts" (p. 69).

The Homestead Acts of the 19th and early 20th centuries in the U.S. and Canada brought new waves of immigrants, enticed by the offer of free land. Although most of the immigrants were of European extraction, few were English speaking. Education was seen as the means of integrating them into the wider society. Bureaucratic and instrumental approaches developed as appropriate ways of organizing schooling to achieve its aim of socializing and assimilating children into North American society.

Educational Administration: Its Roots

Teacher training in North America is as old as the public school movement itself. In fact, Horace Mann is credited with the establishment of the first state-supported "normal school" in Massachusetts in 1839. Normal schools, designed exclusively to prepare elementary school teachers, tended to rely heavily on existing theories of child psychology, while training for secondary school teachers, located from the outset in liberal arts colleges, included a greater emphasis on content areas. Teacher education expanded so rapidly that, by the end of the 19th century, many normal schools had expanded into four-year degree-granting teachers colleges (Borrowman, 1956).

Surprisingly, perhaps, the roots of current thinking about educational administration are almost as old as the trend toward teacher training. In 1875, William Harold Payne, Superintendent of Schools in Adrian, Michigan, wrote the first book on school administration, *Chapters on School Supervision,* with a preface by William Harris, a colleague and Superintendent of Schools in St. Louis (Culbertson, 1988, p. 3). Culbertson writes that Payne:

> Argued that educational organizations are not "objective" phenomena regulated by general laws; rather they are mental constructs that reflect the perceptions and interpretations of their members. Students of organizations should turn their backs, then, upon logical positivistic science and adopt interpretive modes of inquiry. (p. 3)

Indeed, Payne proposed that a "special science be created ... [to] gather and analyze facts and inductively arrive at generalizations about education's ideals" (Culbertson, 1988, p. 5). Harris, head of the Department of Education of the American Social Science Association, "struggled valiantly to accommodate social theory and social practice to the emerging realities of an urbanizing and industrializing society" (Haskell, in Culbertson, p. 5).

Payne and Harris foreshadow the more familiar work of T. B. Greenfield a century later, in calling for a rejection of positivistic views such as those expressed by Auguste Comte in the 1830s and others who followed him. These educators all recognized that educational organizations and those who populate them are not objective phenomena and cannot be reduced to general laws that are derived from observable characteristics and fact-based generalizations.

Perhaps in part because the industrial and scientific norms of the early 20th century were very different from those propounded by Harris and Payne, their insights were overwhelmed by stronger voices. These new theories, advocating the study of observable characteristics of the "real" world, a science of the material and observable rather than the study of and reflection on "moral disciplines," quickly became dominant.

Examinations of early programs in educational administration (rarely called leadership) reveal that most contained a core of courses related to organizational theory, decision making or problem solving, and the practical operation of schools. For most of a century, the preparation of school leaders focused on teaching them things such as how to close the school, handle records, and conduct surveys. Books, articles, and journals disseminated ideas about leading schools and supervising teachers. Practitioners and professors drew their ideas largely from stories of others' experience, essays about topics such as "the joys of administration," information drawn from surveys, and recommendations for improving practice. There was an easy movement between facts and values, between description and prescription. Little thought was given to a need for "improved preparation for school leaders" (Culbertson, 1995, p. 26).

Then, about midcentury, a landmark meeting occurred. Culbertson (1995) explains: "More than fifty professors from twenty leading universities travelled by car, train, and plane to Chicago on November 10, 1957,[2] to take part in a seminar" entitled *Administrative Theory in Education* (p. 34). From

---

[2] 1957 was the year of *Sputnik*, and news articles abounded during the Chicago seminar, increasing the sense of urgency to establish better "science" in the United States.

this seminar, what has become known as the "theory movement" emerged. The movement took much of its inspiration from the thinking of members of the Vienna Circle, a group that strongly believed that "natural science methods can and should be applied to the study of social and human phenomena" (p. 35). These beliefs formed the basis for *logical positivism,* an approach that placed considerable emphasis on "'hypothetical-deductive systems'—sets of postulates, stated in logico-mathematical terms, from which hypotheses could be derived and tested in the real world" (Culbertson, 1988, p. 14). Using the new methods, "even the social sciences, which suffered from much contradictory and fuzzy thinking, could be cleansed and take their place alongside the natural sciences" (1995, p. 370).

Among the other ideas discussed by participants in the Chicago seminar were two books acknowledged by their authors to have been heavily influenced by logical positivism: Simon's (1945) influential *Administrative Behavior* and Halpin's (1958) *Administrative Theory in Education,* a book strongly influenced by Simon. One of the dominant beliefs that emerged from the ideas discussed at the Chicago seminars was that "ought" questions, i.e., questions about ethics and moral purpose or right and wrong, have no place in science and hence lie outside the study and practice of educational administration. Halpin explained: "Theory must be concerned with how the superintendent *does* behave, not with someone's opinion of how he *ought* to behave" (in Culbertson, 1995, p. 41).

With the growing interest in administrator preparation, the proliferation of training programs, and the increasingly perceived need, in the academy, to justify and gain legitimacy for the new field of study, professors of education quickly embraced the new science. In 1958, Thompson reported that members of schools or departments of administration were "forced to defend themselves against charges that they were operating trade schools" (in Culbertson, 1995, p. 45). A scientific approach, they hoped, would help to establish them as theorists and academics and therefore as legitimate members of the academy.

For us, early in the 21st century, our present interest in dialogue is not a concern for the legitimacy of a profession, but for its improvement; moreover, we do not advocate understanding divorced from moral and ethical principles. Almost a century of educational administration and leadership divorced from moral purpose makes our present quest particularly urgent.

Educational Administration: Outside Influences

One further influence must be acknowledged. Interest in studies related to military and industrial organizations, to public administration, and to management theories helped to ensure that the quest for a science of administration was a relatively universal one. Early theorists posited that administrative science must encompass not only educational administration, but all fields of administration. Hence, educational theory drew not only on the thinking of the Vienna Circle and the logical positivist movement in educational administration that originated at the University of Chicago, but on other dominant ideas of the time.

Morgan reports that "much was learned from the military, which since the time of Frederick the Great of Prussia had emerged as a prototype of mechanistic organization" (1997, p. 15). His military reforms, including "the extension and standardization of regulations, increased specialization of tasks, the use of standardized equipment, the creation of a command language, and systematic training ..." (p. 16), can still be easily recognized in the structures of schooling in the early 21st century.

In the early 20th century, Weber (1924) developed some principles related to the legitimate use of authority in an attempt to redress some of the problems of corruption and patronage he perceived to exist in organizations of his day. Hence, he advocated rules for governing a "bureaucratic administrative staff" (p. 5). Among them, he promoted having a specified sphere of competence, a hierarchical organization in which each "lower office is under the control and supervision of the higher one" (p. 6), the separation of ownership from the "means of production" (p. 7), and the need to formulate and record *in writing,* decisions and rules, even if orally determined, that constitute "the office" (p. 7).

Other dominant influences on studies of management, and hence leadership, came from industrialists and management theorists whose body of work, now known by the terms "scientific" or "classical" management," has attracted much support and much critique. Among the early influential thinkers was Henri Fayol, a French management theorist who developed 14 "principles of management" many of which are still prevalent in management theories. He focused on the naturalness of division of work, the need for authority and responsibility to go hand in hand, the importance of unity of command and unity of direction, and the need for fair remuneration. Among his most well-known principles, perhaps, is the scalar chain, a hierarchical line of command that ensures appropriate "line of authority" (1916, p. 267). Less commonly cited is his insistence that written communication may be abused and that there is less potential for differences and misunderstanding if communications are verbal (p. 273)—a topic that perhaps foreshadows the importance of dialogue to be explored in the rest of this book.

One of the most important (and perhaps most damaging) influences of scientific management came from the work of the American engineer Frederick Taylor and his colleague Frank Gilbreth. Their studies of work, based on empirical studies of handling pig-iron, shovelling, and brick laying, are now well known.[3] From them, Taylor deduced four principles of scientific management. The first was that managers needed to take on the task of gathering knowledge and reducing it to rules and applications that may be monitored scientifically. Secondly, the manager must scientifically select, and progressively develop, the workmen. Third, the manager must bring together the knowledge and the worker so that the workers will "cooperate in doing their new duties" (Taylor, 1912, p. 278). Last is the insistence that the manager's work be as taxing and exacting as the worker's; i.e., that "there is hardly a piece of work done by any workman in the shop which is not preceded and followed by some act on the part of one of the men in management" (p. 278). Taylor was, moreover, convinced that "the law is almost universal... that the man who is fit to work at any particular trade is unable to understand the science of that trade without the kindly help and cooperation of men of a totally different type of education ..." (p. 281). In other words, the worker is too stupid to understand the work in which he is engaged and needs constant supervision and direction.

The vestiges of these scientific management theories are clearly evident in much management and leadership practice today. Indeed, they permeate the policies, practices, and processes of public education in North America. Consider, as an example, that the No Child Left Behind Act of 2001, which reauthorized the Elementary and Secondary Education Act, calls for the use of "scientifically based research" as the foundation for many education programs and for classroom instruction.

A publication of the National Research Council (Shavelson & Towne, 2002) set out six (now highly controversial) principles for scientific research. These principles, with their emphasis on replicability and generalizability,

---

[3]   See Taylor, 1912, pp. 280–293, for a first hand description of them.

have caused many to bemoan what they see as yet another illustration of the misapplication of rationality and mechanization to education. [4]

Consider also the proliferation of new programs, always marketed as "best practice," sometimes even as "teacher-proof"—programs to teach reading by phonics, whole language, or balanced literacy; programs to teach math by problem solving or using "manipulatives"; programs to address learning difficulties by patterning, chunking, repeating, recording, etc. New emphases in both Canada and the United States on teacher testing, on high-stakes accountability tests, and on professional standards and recertification are all predicated on notions of scientific management, on the need to monitor and tightly control the practices of teachers and school administrators. Based on assumptions lingering from scientific management, an emphasis on rules rather than relationships and understanding in dealings like Principal Strong had with the parent and student in his office are all considered routine, fair, appropriate, and just, in that they treat everyone in exactly the same way.

Educational Administration in "Tension"

The prevalence of practices that bear resemblance to tenets of scientific management might suggest to the educator unfamiliar with the historical development of educational administration in North America that the movements we have described have been direct and uncontested since the 17th century. Despite their dominance in much of the thinking of the Western world, there have always been other quiet voices calling for more balanced approaches. We have seen how, in the 19th century, the voices of Payne and Harris emphasized the need to include philosophical reflection. Indeed, Harris approached the task holistically, urging "inquiry into education as a whole and comparative study of the 'ideals' of civilizations" (in Culbertson, 1988, p. 5). Even though their early influences were overridden by scientific management and logical positivist movements, counter voices have never been totally silenced.

Consider how different this excerpt from Chapter 19 of Mary Parker

---

[4] The principles are that research must: 1. Pose significant questions that can be investigated empirically; 2. Link research to relevant theory; 3. Use methods that permit direct investigation of the question; 4. Provide a coherent and explicit chain of reasoning; 5. Replicate and generalize across studies; and 6. Disclose research to encourage professional scrutiny and critique (Shavelson & Towne, 2002).

Follett's (1918) *The New State* sounds from the hierarchical, domineering attitude of Taylor (her contemporary management theorist):

> A man said to me once, "I am very democratic, I thoroughly enjoy a good talk with a working-man." What in the world has that to do with democracy? Democracy is faith in humanity, not faith in "poor" people or "ignorant" people, but faith in every living soul. Democracy does not enthrone the working-man, it has nothing to do with sympathy for the "lower classes"; the champions of democracy are not looking down to raise any one up, they recognize that all men must face each other squarely with the knowledge that the give-and-take between them is to be equal. (n.p.; see full-text version accessed on Web)

If educators had taken up her approach to democratic management rather than that of Fayol and Taylor, the principal's response to Mrs. Davis at the beginning of this chapter might have been a quite different, give-and-take interaction. One might suspect this choice was because Mary Parker Follett was a lone voice crying in the wilderness, but this was not the case. She was one of many who tried to temper and challenge the excesses of rational and hierarchical approaches to leadership.

Subsequent movements, such as the human relations and human resource approaches, while instrumental in that they attended to the welfare, comfort, and satisfaction of workers *in order to* achieve increased productivity, also foreshadowed more current approaches to respectful and inclusive management strategies. Mayo (1949), reporting on the need for greater attention to the human dimension and one's need for emotional release, recounts the poignant story of a worker who was interviewed in a study by a member of his research group:

> One worker two years before had been sharply reprimanded by his supervisor for not working as usual: in interview [sic] he wished to explain that on the night preceding the day of the incident his wife and child had both died, apparently unexpectedly. At the time he was unable to explain; afterwards he had no opportunity to do so. (p. 362)

While this situation is certainly more dramatic than the incident with which this chapter opened, there are similarities. Taking a purely instrumental, rational, or bureaucratic approach to one's position may lead to the total neglect of fundamental human needs. But, more than 50 years ago, studies (by Mayo and Roethlisberger) of experiments and interventions at the Hawthorne and Western Electric companies (now known as the Hawthorne Effect) demonstrated that paying attention to something, even if conditions are not actually improved, can make a significant difference.

Scientists, too, have rarely perpetuated a "purely" technical approach to the world. Einstein, for example, in 1931 said the following, in a speech at the California Institute of Technology:

> It is not enough that you should understand about applied science in order that your work may increase man's blessings. Concern for the man himself and his fate must always form the chief interest of all technical endeavors; concern for the great unsolved problems of the organization of labor and the distribution of goods in order that the creations of our mind shall be a blessing and not a curse to mankind. Never forget this in the midst of your diagrams and equations. (p. 312)

Einstein's "concern for the man himself" and Follett's focus on an equal "give-and-take" appear to have more in common with humanistic, critical, or postmodern perspectives than those we have come to associate with a rational and mechanical Cartesian-Newtonian view of the world.

Perhaps most significantly, about 100 years after Harris and Payne had emphasized a phenomenological approach to educational administration, T. B. Greenfield presented a provocative paper that soundly critiqued the theory movement and rekindled the call for integrating facts and values and for acknowledging that organizations are subjective creations of individuals. One of his major contributions was in redefining theory as "sets of meanings which people use to make sense of their world" (Culbertson, 1995, p. 175). He argued that "we live in separate realities" but also that "we live with each other" (Greenfield & Ribbins, 1993, p. 88) and therefore that "if we are to understand organizations as containing multiple meanings, we must abandon the search for the single best image of them" (p. 89).

Implications of Greenfield's critique reverberated throughout the field of educational administration and set off a series of incisive and often acerbic debates, the first of which was a rebuttal by Griffeths (1979). The importance of the critique begun in what have become known as the Greenfield-Griffeths debates is one indication of the power of dialogue to achieve greater clarity and understanding and to learn from alternative perspectives.

The State of the Field, Early 21st Century

Where then does the field of educational administration and leadership find itself at the beginning of the 21st century? Perhaps the simplest answer is the one provided by Donmoyer (1999): we are in a "big tent"—one large enough to encompass the diversity of approaches, strategies, beliefs, values, assumptions, epistemologies, and ontologies that all those who are interested in educational administration and leadership can embrace. Donmoyer writes:

> In the political world, big tent politics involves individuals and organizations (political parties, for example) supporting proposals with contradictory goals in an effort to garner broad-based support and build winning coalitions. ... There are many [...] indicators that an academic version of big tent politics has become a virtual standard operating procedure within the educational administration field. (pp. 31–32).

He then goes on to suggest that although it appears as though most members of the field of educational administration are reluctant to abandon the comfort of their "big tent," it would be desirable for them to find ways to talk "about seemingly intractable problems with those who think and talk differently than they do" (p. 40). While Donmoyer does not use the word *dialogue*, he certainly foreshadows the need for those who advocate different understandings and perspectives to come together in an attempt to understand each other and to address some of the most critical questions of our time. Moreover, adopting the "big tent" solution is easy. Finding ways to interact across difference is considerably more difficult.

We can readily admit that, although we may not completely identify with mechanistic metaphors or prescriptive, technical solutions to educational problems, there is still a propensity for relatively simplistic, atheoretical, quick-fix methods for educational leaders, approaches that still focus on the rational rather than the ethical, on the mechanical rather than the moral purposes of the institution of public education.

Another insight, perhaps less simplistic than some of the foregoing, is offered by cognitive science. Relying heavily on insights from psychology, the cognitive approach tended to highlight individualistic leadership—the skills and the expertise acquired by a single person to permit him or her to come to grips with the best solution to a problem. Hallinger, Leithwood, and Murphy (1991) in their introduction to a book of collected papers presented at a conference held at Peabody College, Vanderbilt University, wrote, "We believe that a cognitive perspective offers the opportunity to better understand the means and processes by which leaders exercise vision" (p. 1). In a later chapter in the same volume, Bolman and Deal (1991) identified numerous strands of thought that come within the "tent" of cognitive perspectives, including schema theory, schemata, representations, cognitive maps, paradigms, social categorizations, attributions, implicit organizing theories, and others (p. 22). Glidewell (1991), in his contribution to the volume, states, "Humans put faith in *cognitive models,* developed over years of confirmation" (p. 34). Leithwood and Steinbach (1991) distinguished between "expert" and "typical" problem-solving expertise in the following way:

> Higher levels of expertise were associated with a larger stock of domain-specific knowledge and more refined skills in planning for group problem-solving and assisting staff in being as productive as possible during their deliberations; this was accomplished through clarifying, synthesizing, and summarizing activities during those deliberations. Finally, dispositions associated with greater group problem-solving expertise included at least the *overt* management or control of intense personal moods, a high regard for staff's potential contribution to problem-solving, and habits of reflection and evaluation of one's thinking and practices. (p. 125)

One sees, in this collection of papers and descriptions of cognitive processes of educational leaders, indications of complex and potentially conflicting approaches. Particularly in the Leithwood and Steinbach quote, one sees evidence of some awareness of the potential importance of human emotions, yet, clearly, they are to be *managed* for the quality of the problem-solution to be achieved.

If the school principal had "managed" Mrs. Davis' distress at her husband's departure and then encouraged her to reflect on the need for her son's suspension, it is unlikely she would have left feeling any more valued, comforted, or included. Without an intrinsic regard for her *as a person*, there would be no need for the outcome of the decision to be any different.

Cognitive approaches to educational leadership, whether they take a fundamentally rational orientation or, as Bolman and Deal (1991) suggest, they include the symbolic and political as well (p. 22), are certainly popular within the "big tent" of educational administration. So, too, increasingly are three perspectives to be briefly discussed in the subsequent section. With so many ways to think about educational leadership, it is no wonder that, for many people, the tent is becoming overcrowded; for many others, the mix is simply too uncomfortable; for still others, the accommodation is untenable.

To help resolve the issue, Joe Murphy (1999), in an invited address for Division A of the American Educational Research Association in Montreal, called for a new "centre of gravity" (p. 44). After examining three possible contenders for the task of unifying the field—democratic community, social justice, and school improvement—Murphy selected school improvement, saying that it "as a principle of correspondence has a broader appeal, that it is more accessible, to the practice and policy domains of the profession" (p. 55) and that it links more closely with his own "research based understanding of school administration and educational leadership" (p. 55).

When advocating a center, Murphy makes the (to us) puzzling comment that "in the world of ideas, diversity is not in and of itself a virtue" (p. 51). He then argues that we need to be "sceptical of the viewpoint that a core will only advantage some ideas and marginalize others" (p. 51). And yet, if one rejects Donmoyer's (1999) "big tent" in favor of a new center, we wonder how it could possibly be otherwise. Some ideas will of necessity be pushed to the margins, perhaps to disappear forever; hopefully those who hold such ideas will fare better in our school communities. Somehow, when one carefully examines Murphy's suggestion for a new center, it becomes apparent that it is not "new" at all; in fact, it is firmly grounded in rational and technical constructs of school effectiveness and school improvement that were popularized during the 1970s and 1980s.[5] Yet Murphy claims that it is somehow more appealing and more accessible than the alternatives he has briefly considered and rejected. Perhaps because the "new center" seems so lack luster, so "old," there have been numerous conference presentations, papers, chapters, and articles critiquing Murphy's approach.

As we examine some of the challenges proffered to the concept of a center, the reasons for our belief in the importance of dialogue and dialogic leadership will become clearer.

De-Centering Educational Leadership

Although there are many important contributions to the de-centering of educational leadership as a rational, technical activity, we will focus here on only a few. Each contributes in a meaningful way to our contention that dialogue is central to a new approach to leadership. First is the challenge, sometimes called "new science" (Wheatley, 1993), that comes to the social sciences from the "pure sciences" themselves. Next are ways in which "postmodernism" has challenged the field, offering multiple new perspectives and critiques rather than the simplicity of a unitary one. Finally, in this section, we examine the challenges related to the two possibilities

---

[5]   See for example the work of Brookover and colleagues (1979), Clark, Lotto, & Astuto (1984), Good & Brophy (1985), and Purkey & Smith (1983).

Murphy rejected, challenges that come primarily from what one might call "critical theory" or at the very least "critical perspectives." In the space of a few pages, the theoretical complexity of each of these ideas will be so simplified that theoretical purists might find it difficult to recognize the fields being described here. Nevertheless, we believe that even a cursory overview will help to elucidate new directions in which educational administration or leadership may find inspiration and wisdom, guidance for what often seems like the daunting and thankless task of educating our children.

Relationships: The "New" Science

As previously noted, there never really was such a thing as pure, objective science. To some extent, the notion of "pure science" has been perpetuated as much by social scientists as by those who worked in "hard" science fields such as quantum physics or chaos theory. A number of people have noted that a mechanistic understanding of the world is more appropriate for stable environments, dominated by certainty and predictability, but considerably less viable in times of social upheaval or uncertainty (Morgan, 1997; Zohar, 1997). They point to the concepts of chaos (irregularity in time) or complexity (irregularity in space) as helpful in less stable environments (Cutright, 2001; Lorenz, 1993). Cutright explains that:

> Chaos in the physical sciences is not the random activity that the term's common use suggests. Chaos theory, instead, holds that many seemingly random activities and systems, in fact, show complex, replicated patterns. The behavior of these systems is non-linear, that is, behavior feeds back upon itself and modifies the patterns. (p. 4)

Wheatley (1993) advocates that educational leaders take up the paradoxical notion of the simultaneous complexity and underlying order of chaos theory, that we let go of the need to predict and control and focus instead on the creation of a few guiding principles that may shape an organization and help us to understand the ways in which it is ordered (p. 11). Moreover, she argues, educational leaders can profitably recognize, that we live in a "world where *relationship* is the key determiner of what is observed" (p. 10). She writes:

> Each of us lives and works in organizations designed from Newtonian images of the universe. We manage by separating things into parts, we believe that influence occurs as a direct result of force exerted from one person to another, we engage in

complex planning for a world that we keep expecting to be predictable, and we
search continually for better methods of objectively perceiving the world.... There
are no recipes or formulae, no checklists or advice that describe "reality." There is
only what we create through our engagement with others and with events. Nothing
really transfers; everything is always new and different and unique to each of us.
(pp. 6–7)

The message Cutright (2001), Wheatley (1993), and many others draw,
not from understandings of science based on 17th century physics, but from
the science of our times, is that relationships and engagement with others are
fundamental to our understanding of the world and to our ability to exercise
leadership. For educational leaders, this requires a sea change, a change from
rules to relationships, from products to processes, from policies to people,
from predictability to possibility.

Current understandings of science demonstrate that our knowledge of the
world, indeed the universe, is governed more by integration than separation,
relationships than discrete entities, perspectives than mechanisms. Moreover,
there is an increasing rejection of the primacy of reason and the orthodoxy of
meta-narratives. The postmodern acknowledgment of the existence of
multiple and valid views of reality offers an important counterbalance to
logical positivistic, "modernist" thinking and, again, implies the importance
of dialogue.

The Postmodern Challenge

While it is difficult to offer a simple definition of postmodernism, it is
possible to identify some of the most salient and influential tenets of its
critique of the modernist notion that reality is singular and knowable and that
it is the task of the researcher and theorist to discover and explain it. In
general, the postmodernist believes that reality is constructed, multi-
perspectival, and multitheoretical, such that there can be no one "right"
meaning (English, 2003, p. 13). Postmodernism rejects binarisms such as
true-false, objective-subjective, and right-wrong, suggesting instead that "all
observations are of implicit value and are ethical acts" (p. 14). Post-
modernists are concerned with power, maintaining that theoretical discourses
are "frozen in a language, a culture, and time-power relations" (p. 15).
Hence, they maintain that "truth is constructed rather than discovered and
that it is embedded in systems of power which are not *value-neutral*" (p. 16).

The school administrator or educational leader will intuitively recognize that there is some wisdom (one dare not call it "truth") to this conception of the world. There is no doubt that on a daily basis, she is confronted by people with different views and understandings, each claiming to be right, each clamouring to be heard. She cannot deal with parents, discipline students, or allocate resources without being aware of the power involved in such routine acts; and she is acutely aware of the difficulty of knowing what course of action is "right" or "good" in a given situation. Our recognition that dilemmas are an intrinsic part of the work of the school leader makes us uncomfortable with simplistic interactions between principal and parent, such as the one with which this chapter opened. A postmodern view of the world, with its recognition and validation of difference, may suggest to the school administrator that dialogue is essential to understanding those with whom she works on a daily basis.

We acknowledge that, taken to its extreme, a postmodern perspective of the world does not allow for or require dialogue. It does not acknowledge that some things may be more beneficial than others, some perspectives more useful or comprehensive than others, and some actions more acceptable than others. Taking a purely postmodern perspective is so relativistic that there appears to be no way out. There is no need to discover what the other means; there is no need to attempt to determine where there are common understandings and where people diverge; ultimately, there is no need to interact, for each person's understandings, constructions, and perceptions are equally valid and meaningful. This stance is, of course, antithetical to the notions of relationship that we have already sketched out and it certainly precludes the need for dialogue.

It becomes clear, then, that the recognition of a plurality of perspectives, perhaps even a plurality of "truths" is only a starting point. Weeks (1990) writes:

> If ever-growing social complexity, cultural diversity, and a proliferation of identities are indeed a mark of the postmodern world, then all the appeals to our common interest as humans will be as naught unless we can at the same time learn to live with difference. This should be the crux of modern debates over values. (p. 92)

He goes on to state, "The basic issue can be stated quite simply: by what criteria can we choose between the conflicting claims of different loyalties" (p. 95)? Indeed, if we are to live in community, to understand what it might mean to create schools that are inclusive, respectful, and deeply democratic, we cannot be satisfied to ignore the claims of others, walking through life without attending to their fundamentally social and relational nature.

We are compelled then, it seems to us, to find ways to both sustain individual identities and perspectives and to develop some ways of understanding that permit us to enhance the quality of our lives together. And for the educational leader, our lives together occur, in large part, in the institutions of schooling.

The Critical Challenge

Critical theorists offer a perspective that, although often associated with that of postmodernism in its critique of modernism and its ills, is fundamentally in opposition to it, for critical theory brings its challenge from a particular perspective in order to bring about change. The term "critical theory" was originally coined and used by Horkheimer in 1937 to describe the theoretical program of the Frankfurt School (Peters et al., 2003, p. 3), and although "Horkheimer (1972, p. 221) maintains that critical theory has no specific content but comprises simply a philosophical orientation 'whose business is to hasten developments which will lead to a society without injustice'" (Peters et al., p. 3), it is clear that implicit in the comment itself are some specifics. Critical theorists (whether they look back to their Marxist roots or simply examine its present manifestations), take the position that society is inequitable and unjust and, therefore, that there are some developments that can be identified and introduced to hasten our progress toward socially just ends. The stance is modernist: we can find ways to improve society. The critique, like that of postmodernism, emphasizes that hegemonic uses of power and privilege perpetuate inequity. But it offers new "closed" solutions designed to bring those who have traditionally been excluded from power closer to the center. Hence it tends to replace one set of solutions with another.

Frequently, issues of multiculturalism are associated with critical perspectives, in large part, because there is recognition that children of visible minority groups, from minoritized (other than dominant) cultures, spiritual perspectives, or socio-economic or ethnic groups, are recipients of unequal resource allocation, excluded from full democratic participation in school life, and prevented from involvement in courses and activities that may offer fuller and more optimistic opportunities for "the good life" beyond school. Stephen May (2000) acknowledges (citing Mohan, 1995) that a critical conception of multiculturalism takes as its starting point a notion of culture as a terrain of conflict and struggle over representation.... Rather than present culture as the site where different members ... coexist peacefully, it has to develop strategies to explore and understand this conflict and to encourage creative resolutions and contingent alliances that move [away] from interpreting cultures to intervening in political processes. (p. 6)

Critical perspectives therefore beg solutions; they demand choices between decisions and actions that marginalize and privilege children and those actions and attitudes that provide educational opportunities that are more equitable and inclusive. Critical theorists do, however, connect with postmodernism in the recognition of multiple paths and *truths*, rather than one universalistic *Truth*; they acknowledge the need for moral action but do not imagine that there is only one right way to their identified goal.

As educators, we would not suggest that solutions to inequity and injustice are unnecessary—quite the contrary. We do believe, however, that new solutions can no more be successfully imposed than previous ones. Rather, the starting point needs to be the relationships and understanding that come from dialogue out of which new solutions may emerge.

The Case for Dialogue: A Way Forward

This very cursory examination of some of the historical movements and events and some of the philosophical underpinnings of current thinking and theorizing in educational administration and leadership has only scratched the surface. Nevertheless, it has shown how policy makers have come to emphasize rational and technical solutions in education and suggested why the principal in the opening interaction might well feel justified in handling a disciplinary incident as he did. We know that educators can recount many more examples of ways in which schools tend to treat parents, students, and teachers as objects, without regard for who they are as persons deeply worthy of respect and regard. We have shown that conflicting ideas and perspectives have always been present, sometimes shoving the less popular ideas far into the shadows, but sometimes holding them visibly in a more dynamic tension. We believe the time has come to acknowledge not only the presence of such tension, but its necessity. We invite our readers to reflect on when leading with an emphasis on the rational, technical, and efficient might be called for; but we also urge you to reflect on the many occasions on which other, more human and humane forms of leadership might be more appropriate.

Although we are convinced that *dialogue* as we will be describing, exploring, and developing it in the coming chapters is critically important for educational leaders (and indeed all leaders), we do not presume to suggest that it is the only requisite way of knowing or being, the only approach that is required. We do, however, agree with Kanpol (2000), who writes:

> In order to effect a re-democratization of the social and the educational in this country, a fusion or synthesis must occur between insights offered by critical theory, postmodernism, and liberal spiritualism.[6] More specifically, we believe the response to the issue of balkanization or the irrelevance caused by theories of fractionalization should be to ask and address the heretofore unasked questions; that is, to seek possibilities for radical transformation within a moral and spiritual framework where a critical argument is subsumed in an ethical one. (p. xi)

We, too, are motivated by the need for ethical arguments, for a more deeply democratic social order; we, too, are inspired by the possibilities inherent in the notion of transformation. Regardless of whether one is engaged in critical argument or ethical argument or both at the same time, it requires a deeper and clearer understanding of dialogue than currently exists.

Barbara Thayer-Bacon (2003), in talking about multicultural curriculum, argues that we need to teach "students about situated truths that are qualified by as much evidence as we can offer" (p. 254). She elaborates, urging that we should also teach "students that criteria and standards for judging the evidence we offer changes [sic] over time and can be corrected and improved upon" and "that the world in which we live is a pluralistic world supported by a variety of truths" (p. 254). When we acknowledge the pluralism of today's society and schools, one of the most pressing tasks is to determine how we may also avoid a relativistic "anything goes" approach. To enter into dialogue about what evidence each party brings to bear, about what actually counts as evidence, about how criteria may be understood in their social and historical contests, examined, changed, and improved on over time, is to help our students learn to become thoughtful, critical, and transformative citizens.

To provide a different way of thinking about the need for dialogue and how it might contribute to a more complete, complex, sensitive, inclusive, and deeply democratic form of leadership, we turn now to a fuller consideration of relationships as fundamental to life and dialogue.

---

[6]   Though not a topic we explore here, we consider Kanpol's inclusion of the spiritual provocative and worthy of further exploration by educational leaders. See also Shields, Edwards, & Sayani (2004).

CHAPTER TWO

Dialogue as Relationship

Sonny was a handsome young man for whom my seventh grade French class seemed not only incomprehensible but totally irrelevant. Mine was not the only class Sonny disliked. Other teachers often complained about his lack of effort. His homework was never done; he rarely responded when called upon in class. His slumped posture, tight lips, and vacant glance attested to his total distaste for the whole schooling endeavor. Totally frustrated, but determined to succeed with him, I persisted. I threatened, yelled, cajoled, demanded, ignored him, and gave detentions. I exhausted my repertoire. One day, after a particularly negative exchange, I suggested that rather than serve a detention, he could come to my place for some extra tutoring. To my surprise, he agreed.

Sitting at my dining room table, we began with the intended exercise, conjugating "avoir" and "être." But soon we began to talk. I learned that Sonny was the child of an Indigenous woman and an American service man. He had lived with his siblings, his mother, and her new partner in a small house in a neighboring town. As a punishment for some teenage offense, he had been ostracized by his parents and forced to live in a shed behind his house—in the $^{-}40°$ temperatures of a Labrador winter. To ensure his survival, a social services worker had intervened and moved him to the boarding school dormitory of the school he currently attended.

I was moved. No longer was Sonny simply a disengaged, uncooperative student. He was a person, a young man faced with an untenable family situation, rejected and unsupported, trying not only to survive, but to succeed in a world that had so far been harsh and unkind.

***

I could not change Sonny's family situation. I did not make him into a French scholar. But in the days and weeks and months ahead, we became friends. He stayed with my family at times—ate meals with us, spent holidays with us, even traveled with us. He experienced things he had never known existed; I learned of situations I had only imagined; and together, we began to develop a friendly relationship.

As we talked, we began to understand each other better, and our relationship deepened; as we spent time together, our understanding of each other's needs and perspectives changed. So too did our actions. I became less "teacher"—monitoring, demanding, assessing and instead more "supporter"—counsellor, listener, mentor, and sometimes friend. I pushed less; he worked more. I asked less; he offered more.

In the Introduction, we introduced the idea of dialogue as relationship and as understanding. There we were led into thinking about dialogue, not in its casual or colloquial sense, but as a powerful and deeply personal way of gaining a better understanding of oneself, one's world, and those with whom one comes in contact.

Chapter One presented some snapshots of ways in which organizational and societal thinking have been shaped and have changed over several millennia and how the evolution of trends and movements has influenced current thinking about educational leadership. We noted that in earlier ways of thinking about organizations, there was emphasis on efficiency, bureaucracy, and hierarchy. The relations that dominated were those of control and instrumentality, relations designed to create predictable and stable outcomes. In the human relations approach (related to the work of Mayo [1949] and Roethlisberger [1941]), when early theorists paid attention to the people within organizational life, the focus was on instrumentality, ways in which attending to human needs could improve the efficiency, effectiveness, and productivity of the organization.

We presented these ideas in acknowledgment that thinking about organizational management and leadership has always been complex and, moreover, that previous insights may provide a useful backdrop for achieving a deeper understanding of where we are today and of some of the challenges, opportunities, and possibilities with which we are presented.

Educational leaders are acutely aware of their organizational responsibilities, of the need for the educational organization to survive and to accomplish its goals, even of the importance, at times, of thinking instrumentally. Nevertheless, a purely or excessively instrumental way of thinking about those who make up an organization is generally dehumanizing, cold, and counterproductive. Thus, in this chapter, we present some alternatives to much of the thinking introduced in Chapter One. If organizations are mechanistic and bureaucratic, there is little need to focus on relationships, and consequently, there is no real argument for this book. On the other hand, if we understand human life as fundamentally relational (we are born through and live in human relationships), then we will require a new basis for educational leadership, one we believe is best captured by the term *dialogic relations*. In this chapter, therefore, we develop the *relational* aspect of our approach to dialogue. (See Figure 2.)

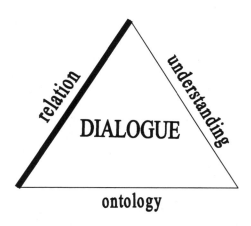

Figure 2. Relational Dimension of Dialogue

The Primacy of Relationships

We have found that in almost every field of endeavor, whether it be the physical sciences or the social sciences, there has been, in recent years, an increased awareness of the nature and importance of relationships. In the next few sections of this chapter, we examine relations in the physical world, then explore the relevance of relationships to human life, and finally develop an understanding of humanity as fundamentally and inherently relational. After having developed the rationale for the primacy of relationships, we spend the rest of the chapter developing the concept of *dialogic relations.*

We need to make it clear from the outset. When we say that relationships are ontological, we are saying that they are a fundamental and intrinsic part of being, that we cannot separate our existence from our relationships. We are not saying that relationships *equal* being, for *being human* comprises more than relationships; but we are saying that relationships are a necessary (but not sufficient) part of living. There is something so important and so fundamental about relationships that we cannot ignore them, even (perhaps especially) in educational settings.

Going against the Grain

Despite the fact that, in the past few decades, we have witnessed much thinking and writing about education, educational accountability, school reform, and educational leadership, the dominant theories and approaches to educational leadership and organizational health have not placed relationships at the center. The current accountability movement in education, designed to ensure that "no child is left behind," neglects the needs of the individual child and focuses instead on performance on norm-referenced standardized tests. Public accountability measures report test results and "league tables," but rarely speak of the quality of the educational environment within which the child is being taught. School reforms emphasize parental rights and choice, but downplay the social fragmentation that such reforms may exacerbate. Teacher testing, intended to provide assurances of the competence of teachers, focuses on their knowledge and skill base, to the neglect of their ability to relate to children. Some have focused on the assessment and identification of leadership skills as demonstrated through in-basket exercises and standardized interview protocols (McCleary & Ogawa, 1989; Richardson & Robinson, 1987). A movement to license school administrators, approved in the United States by several accreditation bodies and 24 states (English, 2003, p. 109), has culminated in a test comprised of "three modules administered in four timed sections" (p. 109) with 25 scored responses. Such accountability measures have ignored the candidate's record for establishing warm, caring, and inclusive school communities within which parents, teachers, and students feel welcomed.

Curiously, as the aforementioned reforms and many other developments in education seem to de-emphasize the importance of relationships, our knowledge of the natural world and its scientific underpinnings is evolving in a different direction: scientists are placing increased emphasis on relations and relationships. The universe is no longer described as one great mechanical clock, set in motion by an unseen but powerful creator, but as a series of systems and subsystems so intricately interwoven that it is difficult, perhaps impossible, to determine where one ends and the other begins. As astronomer James Jeans said in 1942, "Today there is a wide measure of agreement ... that the stream of knowledge is heading towards a non-mechanical reality; the universe begins to look more like a great thought than like a great machine." Many physical scientists, we are told, have come to place pre-eminent importance on relationships, on the "dynamic, living qualities" of the world, and on understanding their patterns of interaction. Wheatley (1993) states that for many scientists, relationships are *all* there is to reality" (p. 32).

Increasingly, there are also other challenges to the worldview that separates humanity and nature, that legitimizes human domination, control, and manipulation of the environment for our benefit, and that ignores our close physical and emotional ties with the world around us. Hampton (in Ward & Bouvier, 2001, p. 7) acknowledged that a "strong relationship to the land, for survival and spiritual renewal, has been considered a defining characteristic of Indigenous cultures." Others within and outside the education system have become aware of the importance of our relationships with the ecosystems within which we live, systems that sustain and nurture us (see, for example, Noddings' [1992] concept of care). Despite the multiplicity of approaches to environmental education, there is growing awareness of the importance of examining the ethical issues related to human-environmental relationships and taking seriously the insights from various bodies of knowledge, including "environmental justice, Indigenous knowledges, feminism and ecofeminism, critical pedagogy, environmental thought, deep ecology, [and] bioregionalism" (Russell, Bell, & Fawcett, 2000, p. 209). When we acknowledge our interconnectedness with natural systems, we recognize that "humans are part of, not separate from, environmental processes" (p. 204).

We are compelled to reflect that if relationships are so central to understanding and explaining the material world, how much more important, then, are relationships to human existence. When we approach the human world, our relatedness to one another does not allow for a clear distinction between *subject* and *object*. On one level, this is the lesson we begin to learn through my interactions with Sonny. Although he never became a passionate or enthusiastic student, he did become, in my French class at least, a cooperative, participating member of the class who ultimately exerted enough effort to achieve a passing grade. Seeing him as an "unruly French student" reduced Sonny to a single dimension; I simplified him, essentialized and objectified him in ways that devalued and dehumanized him. The attitude permitted me to abrogate my responsibility and assume a detached and impersonal stance. Only when I became open to the idea of a different type of relationship (no longer teacher–student, but Carolyn–Sonny) could change occur.

Relational Origins

It is curious that recognition of the importance of relationships has moved to center stage in the physical sciences, but that despite inherently relational beginnings, humans often seem to strive more for independence than for interdependence.

We come into the world in relationship. Joined by an umbilical cord to the one who sustained us through approximately nine months of development, we begin life physically connected to another human being. In fact, without the intervention of other human beings, involved in various types of relations, no human being comes into existence at all. Curiously, despite the self-evidence of this fact, it somehow seems necessary to state.

Buber (1970) wrote, "The longing for relation is primary, the cupped hand into which the being that confronts us nestles; and the relation to that, which is a wordless anticipation of saying You, comes second" (p. 78). Even before we can recognize another person as "You" or "Thou" (as the original translation had it), we are in relationship with the one who nurtures us. Thayer-Bacon reiterates the same concept: "I begin with the assumption that all *people are social beings*. Our lives begin and are lived in relationships with others" (2003, p. 7).

No one doubts that the health and behavior of a pregnant or lactating mother can significantly influence the welfare and development of an infant. Over the years, the adverse effects of a mother's vitamin deficiencies, smoking, or excessive alcohol consumption on her infant have become widely known. We have learned that infections during pregnancy increase infant morbidity rates, may result in lowered birth weight, and, in some cases, cause physical or mental abnormalities.

One wonders why, given our relational origins, so much "science" quickly turns to investigate the processes by which relationships between parent and child are replaced by individual growth, be it the cognitive (Piaget, 1969), social and emotional (Erickson, 1950), or moral (Kolhberg, 1981) development of children. In general, these theories of development rely on notions of increased independence and autonomy: more abstract (rather than concrete or relational) thinking and, in terms of moral development, more "autonomous or principled" decision making (Kohlberg, 1981) are seen as evidence of growth and increased maturity. Gilligan's (1982) critique of the latter in which she challenged the association of increased autonomy with a heightened stage of moral development and emphasized a fundamentally relational human orientation—at least for females—is well known. Despite these well-known and reputed studies, better understanding of individual development has not created happier individuals or a better society.

One could point to numerous statistics related to what many describe as the "breakdown" of the traditional family,[1] the diminution of extended families, and many other social phenomena which support claims that individualism has heightened while social cohesion may be declining. Today's middle-class North American child is enrolled in day care, pre-school, dance, music, and athletic activities long before she has achieved the ability to read or write. Individual performance and achievement have

---

[1] Parents Without Partners, an organization formed to support single parents, reported that in the U.S. 61% of all children will spend all or part of their formative years in a single-parent household, that 16 million children live with only one parent, a number that has doubled since 1970, and that 26% of all U.S. households that contain children under the age of 18 are single-parent households (Parents Without Partners, 2003).

become benchmarks of success.

The critique of an excess of individualism, at least in North American society, is not new. The "communitarian platform," for example, emphasizes the importance of balancing preservation of individual liberty with the need to learn respect for others in a civic society, including learning "to serve others—not just self" (Etzioni, 1993, 253–254).

The authors of the well-known *Habits of the Heart: Individualism and Commitment in American Life*, write:

> Even given the claim that community does not require complete consensus, some people view with skepticism any effort to reach some common agreement about the good. Such a view is rooted in our culture's adherence to "ontological individualism"—the belief that the truth of our condition is not in our society or in our relation to others, but in our isolated and inviolable selves. It is this belief that tempts us to imagine that it is opportunity that will solve all our problems—if we could just provide individuals the opportunity to realize themselves, then everything else would take care of itself. If we focus on individual opportunity then we don't need to worry about substantive agreement or the common good, much less force any such notion on others. Each individual can concentrate on whatever good he or she chooses to pursue. (Bellah et al., 1985, p148)

Our claim, like that of Bellah and colleagues, is that ontological individualism is a distortion of our nature. We argue here the need not for an individual ontology, but for a relational ontology.

Accepting the ontological importance of relationships insists on a balance in which self and others come together in social institutions and daily life, understanding, respecting, and supporting each other, while at the same time never ignoring the rights of the individual within the relationship or society.

Relational Ontology

Although relational ontology may not have found a comfortable home at the center of education, it is a strand of thinking that has permeated much of the philosophical thinking of the past century. Several philosophers, such as Heidegger, Buber, and Noddings, have focused on the importance of relationships, generally on caring relationships, as the basis for our humanity.

The roots of relational ontology in the 20th century can be traced to Martin Buber's statement: "In the beginning is relation—a category of being, readiness, grasping form, mold for the soul" (1970, p. 69). Moreover, he asserts that "all actual life is encounter" (p. 62) and that "only the man who realizes in his whole life with his whole being the relations possible to him helps us to know man truly" (Trapp, 1958, p. 15). To live, according to Buber, is not only to be in relationship, but to turn toward the other, ready to meet him or her where he or she is (p. 67). To live is to care deeply for the other.

This theme of caring is elaborated by Nel Noddings, a prominent philosopher-educator, who states that "caring is a way of being in relation, not a set of specific behaviors" (1992, p. 17). Noddings' emphasis on the affective response leads her to focus specifically on the nature of caring relationships, rather than to engage in a more general exploration of relationships. She believes that educators need to work to develop the "attitudes and skills required to sustain caring relations" (p. 21) and argues that this is more important than the development of moral reasoning. Moral reasoning, she argues, can only take us part way. Knowing the ethical rules and being able to articulate them does not guarantee we will live in harmony one with another; accepting the need to care as fundamental and embedding our words and actions in an ethic of care will take us further. In other words, Noddings says that moral behavior and articulation of the rules of that behavior are not synonyms and she advocates a focus on the former. Indeed, Noddings argues (after Buber) that we need to take "relation as ontologically basic" (1986, p. 4). By this she means that relations are so fundamental to human existence that we cannot be human without them; hence, it is important that we learn to care. Margonis echoes this attitude, calling for an ontological attitude toward educational relationships and arguing that "teachers need to realize that the concern for primacy of relationships in education comes from the realization that relationships have the primacy of being" (summarized by Sidorkin, 2002, p. 86).

Each of these writers implies a concept of relationship that focuses on interactions between and among human beings as foundational to human life. Yet, each also recognizes that such relationships are not always developed and nurtured appropriately. For example, they argue, one may treat another person as if he or she were an object rather than a person, a concept we will explore later when we expand on Buber's critical "I-Thou" and "I-it" distinctions.

There are two other aspects of relations it is essential to mention. One is that relationships are always relations in context; we are not talking about abstract relations, but from birth, the smells, the sight of the blood, the cries of the infant, and the tears of the mother place us firmly in particular times and places, generated by particular cultures, languages, and interpretations of history. In a sense, this is what Freire (2000f) means when he says that to "read the word is to read the world" (p. 163). Understanding cannot happen without reading the world; relationships cannot occur outside the world in which we are situated, whether we are talking about relationships with history, culture, past hurts, new ideas, or other people. Freire expresses this eloquently in talking about liberation; he writes: "Liberation is a praxis; the action and reflection of men and women upon their world in order to transform it" (2000e, p. 73). And he expands this concept with reference to education:

> Education as the practice of freedom—as opposed to education as the practice of domination—denies that man is abstract, isolated, independent, and unattached to the world; it also denies that the world exists as a reality apart from people. Authentic reflection considers neither abstract man nor the world without people, but people in their relations with the world. (p. 75)

For the educational leader, this concept is critical. To create environments in which people may engage in the work of education requires a focus on people in their relations with the world. Eric Fromm (1994) introduces a similar concept. He distinguishes between *having* and *being*, two fundamentally different ways of orienting oneself to the world. Although he makes explicit the potential for human beings to engage in relations that are far from caring or respectful, he also notes the potential to "become one again with man, nature and himself, without giving up the independence and integrity of his individual self" (p. 139). Lankshear and colleagues (2003) summarize Fromm's comments:

> Seek unity in relations with others of domination or submission (authoritarian forms) or by relating equally with them (dialogical or loving forms). We can seek unity through acts of sadism towards others, at one extreme, and by acts of "utter solidarity" at the other. In short, we can pursue unity in so many ways through *having* other people or nature, or through *being* with them. (p. 57)

As educators, we are well aware of the possibility of relating to others in negative and dehumanizing ways; nevertheless, Fromm's emphasis on relating in authentic ways, on getting beyond a *having* orientation to *being* with others, resonates with educators. At the outset, I was involved in a *having* relation with Sonny. I "had" Sonny—a widely known troublesome student—in my class; I had a problem with his unfinished homework; I had a need for him to master the French vocabulary and verb forms and to attain a passing grade. Sonny *had* me as a nagging teacher. I developed a more *being* relationship with him as I learned about his lived experience, his rejection by his family, and his deep longing for acceptance and validation. Regardless of how much I desired or worked toward his *having* success in my class, I failed. But when I changed my focus to engage with Sonny as a person, rather than Sonny as a student of French, Sonny *became* a "success." The distinction is critically important for educational leaders who want to enter into dialogic relationships with those around them and, hence, leads us to an investigation of the nature of a dialogic relation and how it may promote more authentic *being* rather than *having* ways of relating.

Dialogic Relationships

We are all familiar with people who seem to talk without ceasing, but who say very little of any import, making little connection. Educators can readily call to mind the person whose opening words are met with a roll of colleagues' eyes and blank stares, suggesting that, once again, the same old message will be conveyed. As Heidegger said, "To Say and to speak are not identical. A man may speak, speak endlessly, and all the time Say nothing. Another man may remain silent, not speak at all and yet, without speaking, Say a great deal" (in Liston, 2001, p. 50). Speaking endlessly may barely be considered communication; it is certainly not dialogue.

Herein lies some of the complexity of the concept of a dialogic relation. Its fundamental characteristic is meaning, not words. The type of relation we envisage when we think about a dialogic relation is complex and multi-faceted, but always comprises three central ideas. It requires adopting an I-Thou stance to the other. It requires a certain space or distance between self and other. Perhaps most importantly, it begins, not with self, but with other. Let us take each of these in turn to ensure that we understand the basis for a relational orientation to life before we connect relationship to dialogue in the concluding section of this chapter.

I-Thou: A Starting Point

To remind ourselves of Fromm's concept that we can exist in a *having* or *being* attitude toward the world is to begin to understand what Buber (1970) and others mean when they call for distinguishing between relationships between self and others (I-Thou) and between self and inanimate matter (I-It). But more importantly, Fromm reminds us that we often behave in ways that lead to the objectification of other human beings, such that we engage others as if they were objects, dehumanizing them and disrobing them of their rightful position as fellow sojourners on the planet. Buber explains: "*I* and *Thou* exist only in our world, because man exists, and the *I*, moreover, exists only through the relation to the *Thou*" (Trapp, 1958, p. 23).

It is certainly possible, indeed necessary, to relate to the material world as *It*, without need of absolute regard. Further, we know that it is also possible at times to relate to other people as if they were an *It*. Buber acknowledges that "every You in the world is doomed by its nature to become a thing, or at least to enter into thinghood again and again" (1970, p. 69). Nonetheless, it is necessary to affirm the *being* of others in order to know the *being* of oneself. While I-It relationships tend to be instrumental, focusing on things for their utility to help us achieve a desired end (we focus on food when we are hungry or finding shelter when it is raining), I-Thou relationships are of a different and higher order in that they exist to make us real. Buber asserted: "The I is actual through participation in actuality. The more perfect the participation is, the more actual the I becomes" (1970, p. 113). In other words, we become real by virtue of participating as fully as possibly in real life. Hence, relationships are not abstract but material, grounded in the lived reality of daily routines.

Just as our existence originates in relationship and develops in the womb, connected to another, so our being grows and develops through intimate and meaningful relationships in the world. "The *I* of *I-It* relations is an individual differentiated from other individuals" (Thayer-Bacon, 2003, p. 81), while the I of I-Thou relations is an individual connected to others but, paradoxically, living to some extent apart from others. The starting point for such I-Thou relations is our willingness to commit to relational living, a commitment enacted when we engage one another with absolute regard.

When I saw Sonny as teacher to student, I objectified him, seeing him in a narrow and restricted way, limited to my need for him to comply and achieve what was required of him. I failed to see him fully as an individual, a

Thou with unique hopes, desires, aspirations, emotions, and characteristics. When he came to my house and sat across the table from me, I looked into his eyes, perhaps, at times, even glimpsed his heart and soul, and he became "Sonny." I set in motion Buber's concept of sharing as I began to understand and hence share some of Sonny's reality. Buber wrote:

> He who takes his stand in relation shares in a reality, that is, in a being that neither merely belongs to him nor merely lies outside him. All reality is an activity in which I share without being able to appropriate for myself. Where there is not sharing there is no reality. (1953, p. 63)

I did not become Sonny, but together we participated in a new type of interaction, one that had not been possible previously. I became committed to knowing him as a person. I stopped facing him as "teacher"—somewhat disconnected, quite unseeing, unfeeling, unknowing—and instead turned toward him as person, ready to learn from him and about him.

I-Thou: Separate but Connected

I did not become Sonny, but I stood with him in ways I had not previously chosen. The distinction, although obvious in some ways, is also important. What changed were our relative positions. I no longer stood in opposition to him, but *with* him; I no longer sat in "judgment" as teacher-evaluator, but turned toward him in a deeper regard for who he was. Buber calls this "between" "a primal category of human reality" (Trapp, 1958, p. 23). He explains:

> It [language] is rooted in one being turning to another as another, as this particular other being, in order to communicate with it in a sphere which is common to them but which reaches out beyond the special sphere of each. (p. 22)

Paradoxically, dialogical relationship requires distance, what Bakhtin calls "outsideness," a separateness from which Gadamer claims our horizons may fuse. We need to establish a between space in which we meet another in an I-Thou relation. We stand, as those to whom Gibran (1923) speaks of marriage:

> Sing and dance together and be joyous, but let each of you be alone,
> Even the strings of a lute are alone though they quiver with the same music.
> Give your hearts, but not into each other's keeping.

> For only the hand of Life can contain your hearts.
> And stand together, yet not too near together:
> For the pillars of the temple stand apart,
> And the oak tree and the cypress grow not in each other's shadow.

Living in relation to another or to others does not require that we give up our identity. Rather it is imperative that we retain a sense of who we are. In this sense, we stand at a distance, in relation with, but not appropriating, the other. We meet or encounter the other; we do not become the other. Yet, paradoxically, the relation is "unmediated;" as Buber says, "nothing conceptual intervenes between I and You, no prior knowledge and no imagination" (Trapp, 1958, p. 62). Relational dialogue not only requires commitment, but, as Burbules (1993) also noted, it requires reciprocity as well. Roberts (2003), writing about Freire, explains that "the existence of an 'I' is only possible because of the concomitant existence of a 'not-I' (p. 155).

Thus, to enter into dialogue with one whom we acknowledge to be in some ways different from ourselves, we must "encounter" the other person. Buber (1970) posits *encounter*, the ability to stand in relation to another, as key to the possibility of relationship and dialogue. Buber elaborates in less abstract and more graphic language:

> We greet those we encounter by wishing them well or by assuring them of our devotion or by commending them to God. But how indirect are these worn-out formulas ... compared with the eternally young, physical, relational greeting of the Kaffir, "I see you!" or its American variant, the laughable but sublime "Smell me!" (p. 70)

McHenry (1997), commenting on Buber's statement, explains that "smell me" means something like "Distinguish me as a presence. Get me in my strongest particularity" (p. 4). Though bodily confrontation may be met with distaste, with a desire for avoidance, McHenry suggests that it may be a cry for encounter. Sonny's long hair (at a time when it presented a challenge to the school dress code), my elder son's tattoos on his forearms, or the stud in the nose of the waitress in the neighborhood coffee shop may simply be stabs at self-expression. But they may also be attempts at forcing encounter, assertions of the need to be noticed, to enter into I-Thou relations with those who are outside their world.

Sidorkin (2002) puts it another way. He asserts:

> Relations cannot belong to one thing; they are the joint property of at least two things. Relations are located, so to speak, in between things and are located in neither of the things joined into a relation. (p. 94)

He concludes this line of thinking by saying that existence is "an honor, bestowed by others; it is impossible to achieve on your own" (p. 94). Thus, to bestow the honor of existence on another, we need to reflect carefully on ourselves, the nature of the space between us, and the other himself or herself. As we will see, dialogue is the interaction that permits communication across the spaces; it permits discernment.

Relationship: Begins with Other

One of the most common maxims of relationship is that known as the "Golden Rule": *Do to others that which you would have them do to you.* The dictum offers a basis for ethical behavior in relationships, yet there is a sense in which it also implies a selfish and hegemonic attitude. It seems to suggest that if I do to others what I want them to do to me, I know what is best for them. It implies that what I want done for me is also right for them. Yet, for a dialogic relation to occur, it is important to start, not with self, but with other. It is critical to turn one's focus from oneself, to turn toward the other in absolute regard, and to attempt to understand what it is that he or she needs or wants, never assuming that what is right for I is also right for Thou.

McHenry (1997) expresses a similar concept when he writes about Heidegger:

> Martin Heidegger (amongst others) has let us notice how inexorable the Cartesian starting-point has become—"What is more indubitable," he asks archly, "than the givenness of the 'I'?"—and points to the consequences which attend on starting at this point. For starting with this givenness, he says, leads us to "disregard everything else that is 'given—not only a 'world' that is, but even the being of the other 'I's." Once we separate subject from object, once we interpret the cogito as the activity of solitary consciousness reflecting on its environment, we have boarded a boat destined to sail in a single ocean. (p. 2)

The point is that starting from oneself does not permit absolute regard for the knowledge, rights, and perspective of the other; instead, it assumes the superior wisdom of the I with which one starts. Starting with I led me to believe that I knew how to help Sonny pass his French course. Starting with Sonny led me to points I had not anticipated, an understanding of his family situation, and conversations about his future.

When we get beyond ourselves, beyond even the maxim of the Golden Rule, we become aware that we cannot impose any attitudes, even ones of acceptance or openness or tolerance toward others. We can only bring to our interaction with another person absolute regard, without preconceived solutions for "their problems." When another person meets my openness with his or her own, a dialogic relation begins. Such dialogic relationships, at a very fundamental level, are creative; they facilitate changing, growing, and learning—about ourselves and about the other.

Buber (1970) uses the mystical term "grace" to describe the relationship: "The You encounters me by grace—it cannot be found by seeking" (p. 62). I can be open to the other, but only as the other is also open to me can relationship occur. It cannot be forced, merely anticipated. I can and must remain open; I can offer the possibility of a dialogic relation, but until Sonny responds, a dialogic relationship does not occur. The reciprocity essential to dialogic relations is still missing. Moreover, such a relationship does not occur full blown, all at once when one turns toward the other; it may develop slowly, carefully, as my openness permits the other to trust, to open a little, to trust more, and to open still further. The possibility of a dialogic relation relies on my being open, but dialogue can only occur when the other joins in the process.

Dialogic Relationships: The Heart of the Matter

Buber writes that "the relation in education is one of pure dialogue" (Trapp, 1958, p. 23). Buber leads us to believe that relationships are fundamental to our human existence and, hence, ontological. With him we believe that an I-Thou relationship is constituted by dialogue, thus, that dialogue is also fundamentally ontological. Buber here expressed a key idea: the centrality of dialogue for education. Conceptualized in this way, dialogue is no longer talk, no longer a strategy or a method, but a way of being.

This is the quality of dialogue we want to explore here: its potential to support, create, and enhance life itself. Educational leaders who ground their practice in this type of thinking will no longer be overwhelmed by the continuous parade of new programs, policies, or accountability measures. Although these are important considerations for a school administrator, they are not the primary focus.

The priority becomes praxis that enhances relationship and understanding. Further, it will be action grounded in trust and absolute regard for the other. Buber explains that genuine dialogue,

> no matter whether spoken or silent—[is] where each of the participants readily has in mind the other or the others in their present and particular being and turns to them with the intention of establishing a living mutual relation between himself and them. (p. 19)

Bakhtin (1984) expands this notion of living mutual relations. He describes both what it entails and how one goes about entering into this type of relation: with one's whole life. He asserts:

> To live means to participate in dialogue: to ask questions, to heed, to respond, to agree.... In this dialogue a person participates wholly and throughout his whole life: with his eyes, lips, hands, soul, spirit, with his whole body and deeds. He invests his entire self in discourse, and this discourse enters into the dialogic fabric of human life. (p. 293)

We can no more live fully without dialogue than we can come into existence without relationships. Moreover, participation in dialogue is not something one takes up casually, on occasion, but in which one must invest wholly and continuously if one is to participate abundantly in life. Freire (2000a) expresses a belief that is very similar:

> Dialogue is an I-Thou relationship, and thus necessarily a relationship between two Subjects. Each time the "thou" is changed into an object, an "it," dialogue is subverted and education is changed to deformation. (p. 89)

Freire's terms are important for educators whose fundamental purposes are *transformation* rather than *deformation*. Moreover, they constitute a solemn reminder that when we objectify our students, treating them more like objects, reducing them to one or two simplistic ideas, we fail to enter into relation with them. We treat them, at best, as simplified subjects, as two-dimensional people. We change the face of education and distort, subvert, and deform it.

For these theorists, dialogue is fundamental to both life and human interaction, and thus, it becomes possible to assert that dialogue is ontological. Bakhtin elaborates this understanding of dialogue as relational and ontological by introducing two sets of opposing concepts: *monologism* and *dialogism*, and *langue* and *parole*.

Monologism is the term he uses when an "utterance" (a statement that reflects the individuality of the speaker) is unidirectional, when it is either describing relations among objects or between a person and an object or when we "de-personify" the other, while dialogism is the creative interaction that generates meaning reciprocally. Swingewood (1998) distinguishes between them in this way:

> Monologism conceives the other as finished, complete, an object of consciousness, while dialogism celebrates the unfolding, unfinished consciousness which lives only through its relations with others. Monologism leads to a turning inwards ... dialogism abhors enclosure, turning outwards to encounter and respond to the consciousness of others. (p. 115)

Monologism, when used in relation to other human beings, essentializes them and robs them of meaningful personhood. Dialogue is fundamentally concerned with making meaning. Dialogue is understanding and understanding is dialogue according to this interpretation of the term. Bakhtin (1986d) states this clearly: "The relation to the thing ... cannot be dialogic.... The relation to *meaning* is always dialogic. Even understanding itself is dialogic" (p. 121).

In this quotation, Bakhtin introduces the inextricable connections between dialogism, relationships, and understanding—the making of meaning. This introduces the concept of understanding, the dynamic we take as the second key dimension of dialogue. Here, we simply introduce the topic. In the next chapter, we draw on the work of Gadamer and others to further elaborate it.

Dialogic relations are always unique, always complex; they can be neither predicted nor contained. They bear little similarity to some of the diagrams, signs, and symbols often used to describe communication in terms of senders, the message, the medium, and receivers, for these are all monologic terms describing objects. Indeed, Bakhtin (1986c) calls this approach to communication "scientific fiction" (p. 68). Hence, his focus is not on what he calls *langue*, a linguistic system that conceptualizes language as a system of rules and relations, as syntax and morphology, as devoid of its social and historical context; his emphasis is on *parole*. *Parole* is a living, breathing contextual, and evolving way of thinking about language and communication. By this conception,

> Meaning belongs to a word in its position between speakers ... realized only in the process of active, responsive understanding. Meaning does not reside in the word ...

[but] in the effect of interaction between speaker and listener. (Bakhtin & Volosinov, 1973, p. 95)

Words, in and of themselves, are meaningless. Unless we know we share an understanding of what a given word or phrase means, unless we know the tone with which it is spoken, the context in which it is situated, we cannot create meaning or understanding. This is the notion of *addressivity* posited by Bakhtin (1986c). He explains:

> When speaking I always take into account the aperceptive background of the addressee's perception of my speech; the extent to which he is familiar with the situation ... his views and convictions, his prejudices ..., his sympathies and antipathies—because all this will determine his active responsive understanding of my utterance (p. 95–96)

When I treat Sonny as a student of French, telling him he must complete his homework, apply himself, and study harder, I am not engaging in dialogue with him, but am involved in a monologic utterance that disrespects him and disregards his right to share his interpretations, his meanings with me. I am paying absolutely no attention to his context, his needs as a human. I am, in fact, treating him as an object with which I am interacting in a fixed, closed way. As Freire might put it, I have changed education to deformation because I have subverted the possibility for dialogue.

On the other hand, if I engage in dialogue with Sonny about his unfinished homework, I hear his mumbled "I did not do it" in a new way. I need to know more. *Why* did he not do his homework? What was his context? What was going on in his life? I treat him as a person (instead of an object), and together we make sense of the situation. Thus, the possibility is there for me to learn that he did not do his homework because he had been consumed with finding something to eat and a place to sleep. In a dialogic relation, I can no longer be dogmatic, certain that I know best. Rather, as Bakhtin (1986a) says, I "must not reject the possibility of changing or even of abandoning [my] already prepared viewpoints and positions"(p. 142).

Communication between people, between what Freire calls "Subjects," is primary; there is no medium between them. Bakhtin (1986d) states:

> With *explanation* there is only one consciousness, one subject; with *comprehension* there are two consciousnesses and two subjects. There can be no dialogic relationship with an object, and therefore explanation has no dialogic aspects (except formal rhetorical ones). Understanding is always dialogic to some degree. (p. 111)

Not even words, phrases, sentences, or language itself comes between two people and the comprehension that *dialogue* helps them to achieve. Dialogue therefore transcends language; it permits a direct relation between individuals. To return to Buber's concept, we "very well may experience the world of *It* only through language, but we meet *Thou* directly" (Sidorkin, 1999, p. 26). The meeting may not be easy. Buber (1970) himself noted that it may involve sacrifice and risk, but he believed the commitment was still important:

> The deed involves a sacrifice and a risk. The sacrifice; infinite possibility is surrendered on the altar of the form …. The risk: the basic word can only be spoken with one's whole being: whoever commits himself may not hold back part of himself…. (p. 60)

Although there are no recipes for successful dialogue, Burbules (1993) does propose three rules: participation, commitment, and reciprocity (p. 79–83). While we caution that "rules" may introduce a ring of prescription and technicism that is antithethical to dialogue, the rules (we would prefer to call them *guiding principles)* he presents are important. First, although dialogue requires the participation of all members, people need to participate freely and voluntarily and to feel free to remain silent or even to withdraw at times, as necessary. Moreover, they must not participate in such a way as to exclude others or appear to dismiss alternate positions as unworthy of consideration. In other words, treating the other with absolute regard is the starting point for dialogue. Second, all participants must be committed to seeing the interaction through to a point where understanding (although not necessarily consensus) is achieved. The third principle, reciprocity, requires that dialogue be undertaken in a "spirit of mutual respect and concern, and must not take for granted roles of privilege or expertise" (p. 82).

We note here (with Burbules) that relating to the "not-I" may be fraught with challenges, yet difference does not, and must not, preclude dialogue. Indeed, difference is an intrinsic part of it. Dialogue, Burbules (1993) says, requires a "level of reciprocity that binds partners together in a mutual relation of concern and respect (a relation that is fully cognizant of their differences)" (p. 27). He elaborates: in dialogue, one "cannot assume that people will speak the same way, mean the same things, or share the same concerns when they speak (or for that matter will feel safe speaking at all)" (p. 37).

Through dialogue comes infinite possibility, but it also requires unyielding commitment. Meaning is born because an utterance is carefully addressed to someone else and is heard by that someone else. Meaning is not internal to the language; it is not contained within one individual, but is created through dialogue and interaction, through relationships.

Dialogue: The Context

Dialogue, as we have developed the concept thus far, is powerful, personal, intimate, and challenging. Yet one does not, and cannot, always live in dialogic relations. Indeed, it is quite necessary, at times, to engage in monologism. When a school leader gives a speech at an opening school assembly, welcoming students and telling them about the school rules, there is no dialogism present, but the format may be absolutely appropriate. If however, the principal is engaging in similar behavior in her office with upset parents and a student who has broken the rules, monologism is likely inappropriate. Here, discernment is needed in order to determine the best course of action. But understanding is also needed because it is the way in which, to be true to ourselves, we must choose to treat others, to enter into relation with them.

If I am asked to present a keynote address at a major conference, while I may enter into dialogue in advance with those on the organizing committee and with trusted colleagues, developing understanding about the context, the organization, and the message I might opt to deliver, the address itself is not, and likely cannot be, dialogic. Yet, following the keynote speech, it is quite likely that some of the interactions will be dialogic. There may be those who simply compliment me on a "nice speech," while others may stop to say that they agreed or disagreed about a specific point, but choose not to enter into conversation about the point of agreement or conflict. Still, a few may take time for dialogue, inquiring into my meanings and sharing their views and perspectives.

In the latter case, there are two aspects worthy of comment. First is that there must be a degree of trust in order for dialogue to occur. I am unlikely to enter into conversation about the ideas of my talk if I believe the other is closed and has no desire to learn, understand, or grow. Neither am I likely to begin a dialogue if I am closed, believing in the absolute rightness of what I have said, confident that nothing that anyone else might say could influence my thinking in any way. In order for a dialogue to occur, even a relatively superficial one in the context of a keynote address at a conference, there must be some sense of trust, a belief that the other person truly wants to investigate, share, and debate. Hence, a modicum of trust is one of the essential contextual elements for dialogue to occur. Buber (cited in Trapp, 1958) wrote about this in terms of "truth." He stated:

> Whatever the meaning of the word "truth" may be in other realms, in the interhuman realm it means that men communicate themselves to one another as what they are. It does not depend on one saying to the other everything that occurs to him, but only on his letting no *seeming* creep in between himself and the other. It does not depend on one letting himself go before another, but on his granting to the man to whom he communicates himself a share of his being. This is a question of authenticy of the interhuman, and where this is not found, neither is the human element itself authentic. (p. 22)

Trust—or truth—does not depend on having an already deeply established working relationship or friendship with the other person. It does not require spilling everything or sharing beyond what is comfortable. But trust does require that what we share is real, that there is no pretense, no dissimulation, no *seeming* (as Buber called it). Dialogue requires some assurance that each is open to sharing and learning from the other.

For a dialogic meeting to occur, there is no need for us to like each other or to empathize with the other's position. Sidorkin puts it this way: "Dialogue is not empathy and does not imply love or sympathy. What it does imply though is giving the other a full voice, it is taking one's opponent very seriously" (2002, p. 190). For relationships and dialogue to occur, one needs simply to be open to the other, willing to learn, to share, and to develop understanding. We do not need to like the other; we may even see him or her as an *opponent*, but we must treat him or her with absolute regard.

We join with Burbules in emphasizing that engaging in dialogue is something "we learn to do through practice, not by following any sort of recipe or algorithm" (1993, p. xi). His concept of dialogue, like ours, is a fundamentally relational "activity directed towards discovery and new understanding" (p. 8). The relationship may be filled with tension, but it must be one in which the participants are firmly committed to what he calls an "ongoing communicative relationship" (p. 19).

Concluding Comments

In this chapter, we have demonstrated that relationships have been underemphasized in recent theories about education. We have claimed that rather than thinking of relationships as incidental, it behooves the educational leader to consider that relationships are fundamental to life and, hence, to the educational endeavor. We have thus argued that relationships are inherently ontological. They are essential to *being* and certainly to *being human* in this world. We have also made a case for dialogue as the means by which relationships are created, nurtured, and developed. Dialogue, as we have presented it, is not just talk, not just words, not just a means or method for communication, but communication itself. Dialogue permits us to avoid treating others in dehumanizing, disrespectful, deforming ways, as objects, but rather how we enter openly into relationships and communications with others that are respectful and other oriented, seeking to understand rather than to be right, seeking to hear and be heard, rather than to have a predetermined message carefully delivered to its intended audience.

For the school leader, the implications of living in relationship with others, being open to dialogue, learning with and from each member of the school community are significant. Dialogue offers ways of thinking about leading that are far removed from the normal emphasis on rules, programs, and policies that occupy so much of most educators' lives. Dialogue places relationship and understanding at the center rather than the periphery of school life. If one considers dialogue simply as "talk," as a strategy to be learned or a tool for solving problems, then it has been denuded of much of its power and robbed of its potential to create inclusive and deeply democratic school communities.

Changing from managerial to dialogic leadership is not easy. It requires trust, risk, openness, and authenticity to a degree that many school leaders have not considered or encountered. Yet, treating others with absolute regard and developing relations with them offers the potential for empowering, trusting interactions and the basis for meaningful and successful school communities. Dialogic leadership holds the potential to create unity in diversity and to build community amongst a group of disparate individuals. But grounding one's practice in dialogic leadership is also a way to develop greater understanding. Relationship is the first component of dialogue as we conceptualize it. We turn in the next chapter to an investigation of understanding—the second primary facet of dialogue.

CHAPTER THREE

Dialogue as Understanding

I heard them approaching and had just time enough to conclude a phone call and clear my papers from the circular meeting table in my office. Kenny exploded into my office, rage electric in his eyes, face red, a sneer tightly drawn over clenched teeth. He crashed through a couple of chairs to get beyond the table, back to the far wall. A public harangue pursued him through the door, spittle hitting my gesturing hand. "You are finished. Through! I will not have this student in my class or in this school." The slammed door punctuated this final statement. Both glared at each other.

I could see the wide eyes of the waiting parents sitting outside my office just before the door slammed. "I hope they're still there when we've worked this through," I thought.

"I gather there has been a problem," I said, as calmly as I could, and with those words we began the process of understanding.

***

Whenever we are involved in a dialogue with another, we learn, we gain insight, we understand. As we have argued with regard to dialogue's relational dimension, every true dialogue will be characterized by understanding. But what, precisely, do we mean by this and why should dialogical understanding be foundational to the lives and leadership of educators?

Dynamics of Understanding

Understanding, Hans-Georg Gadamer (2002) has argued, is fundamental to human existence. Whenever we seek to make sense of another person's meaning, we are engaged in the process of understanding. When we understand, we have included in our own thinking the meanings of another. When we are understood, another has rightly included our own meanings in her thinking. These ideas of Gadamer resonate strongly for us, and hence, his theory of understanding informs much of our thinking about dialogue as understanding elaborated in this chapter (see Figure 3).

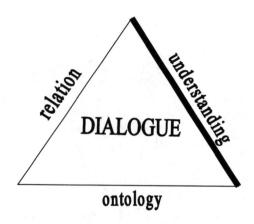

Figure 3. Understanding Dimension of Dialogue

We know we understand when the other person confirms that we have accurately reflected back what was meant. We know we are understood when the other accurately represents what we meant. This experience everyone has shared. When one person explains where he lives and the other person explains how to get from there to her house, his successful arrival indicates their mutual understanding. The experience of understanding may be simple and prosaic. And yet, the experience of understanding and being understood may also be thrilling and life changing, forming the basis of lifelong friendships, marriages, collaborative working relationships, or student–teacher connections that are never forgotten. In part, this range of experience is accounted for by the topic under consideration—a street address versus a person's cultural identity, for instance. But the range of human experience of understanding is also a consequence of how deeply the process of understanding itself is understood and engaged.

In this chapter, we clarify what we mean by *understanding*, depict some dynamics of understanding, establish how we may engage understanding more deeply, and suggest the possibilities and significance of this aspect of dialogue for educational leadership. To give a brief thumbnail sketch, understanding occurs in a to-and-fro movement, or play, of significations between participants. Each participant is open to the other's meanings. In the back-and-forth process of query and response, participants confirm that the other has accurately understood what was meant. As understanding grows in participants, each will expand his or her perspective of a topic (or topics) to include the perspective of the other participant(s). New knowledge results.

The "Play" of Significations

It would be great if we could provide a recipe for educational leaders outlining the steps to achieve understanding among people, a "scientific" method that would produce another's "truth" with every application of the recipe. Unfortunately, this is not possible because developing understanding and being understood are dramatically influenced by those engaged in the process. No single recipe applies. Gadamer observes that understanding develops in a process best depicted metaphorically as "play" (2002, p. 102). Of "play," he writes:

> If we examine how the word "play" is used and concentrate on its so-called metaphorical senses, we find talk of the play of light, the play of the waves, the play of gears or parts of machinery, the interplay of limbs, the play of forces, the play of gnats, even a play on words. In each case what is intended is to-and-fro movement that is not tied to any goal that would bring it to an end.... The movement backward and forward is obviously so central to the definition of play that it makes no difference who or what performs this movement. (p. 103)

Gadamer further elaborates how in the process of play, players lose themselves. One may recognize here how an intensely played game causes one to think of nothing else, but Gadamer wants us also to note that beyond this psychological experience of losing ourselves in a game, there is a sense in which the game plays the players.

Our own experiences reinforce the importance of this "to-and-fro" movement. Imagine walking into a classroom prepared to engage the topic of racism and limiting the play of significations to one sentence by the teacher and one sentence by one student. Or attempting to discover why one's child is upset and ten seconds into the conversation to have the phone go dead. We clarify meanings, sharpening our understanding of what another thinks, through an often intense back-and-forth engagement that plays us even as we respond and listen. The length of time, the context of the interaction, and the commitment of participants to the engagement will strongly influence the level of understanding attained.

When we reflect back on our own experiences of dialogical understanding gained with another, we note how the to-and-fro movement of meanings does not occur all at once, but rather over a period of hours, days, months, even years. Similarly, the context of this play may include formal settings, such as school offices and classrooms, and informal settings such as social events and intentional retreats. The circumstances may span casual, informal conversations and formal meetings or shared investigations. But, across whatever span of time and variety of contexts and circumstances, a commitment to engage the other's meanings is present. As educational leaders, our capacity for, and commitment to, creating situations where the "play" of significations may occur freely will profoundly influence the possibility of understanding and being understood, not just between ourselves and those with whom we work, but also throughout our educational communities.

In the case of the raging student and teacher that opened this chapter, the sort of "play" of significations, or back and forth movement of meaning that the principal enables, will have a powerful effect on how this incident works out. Likely, at first, both teacher and student will attempt to limit any further play of meanings, neither wanting to consider the other's point of view. Initially, the principal must allow the to-and-fro interaction to occur between herself and each of the participants. If she were to stop this fragile play too soon, her understanding of the salient factors of this incident would be diminished, and the participants might feel that she had not understood their situation sufficiently to engage the problem appropriately. Further, enabling a rich "play" of significations has the effect of providing the possibility for each participant to cultivate some self-understanding with regard to the incident. The principal's careful desire to develop understanding of the incident and of the persons involved provides each participant with some trust that the eventual outcome will be reasonable and acceptable. Keeping in mind the importance of developing understanding between the student and the teacher if reconciliation is to occur, framing opportunities for the respectful to-and-fro of their perspectives and meanings will be crucial.

The opportunity to "play" is a necessary dynamic for understanding to occur. Gadamer (2002) observes that the "play" of significations that develops understanding may never end, that what is being understood may always require a further reflection and response. Moreover, though we would like the "play" to work toward a purpose, as in the case of the student and the teacher, Gadamer argues that such "play" is not goal oriented. We may think our to-and-fro is a means to an end, but once engaged, this "play" takes us beyond our intentions. Thus, even when a decision is needed or an action required, we remain open to unanticipated possibilities for new meanings and understanding.

Being Open

Gadamer (2002) explains it this way:

> All that is asked is that we remain open to the meaning of the other person or text. But this openness always includes our situating the other meaning in relation to the whole of our own meanings or ourselves in relation to it. (p. 268)

In the "relationship" chapter earlier, we built on our experience and on theory to elaborate a relational conception of openness based upon an ethical imperative to address the other with absolute regard. This openness, we suggested, is founded upon every person's inherent claim to be considered a "Subject" (Freire, 1983) or a "Thou" (Buber, 1970)—an equal with inherent and intrinsic worth. The openness to another person which we wish to elaborate further in this section begins with this turning toward the other—an encounter, Buber called it. Such a turning commits us to hearing the other's voice in his or her alterity, according to how she or he wishes to be understood. But opening our mental models and frameworks to consider the other's meanings in their difference is no simple task, and it is to an exploration of how this can be done to which we now turn.

Opening our cognitive frameworks to engage another's meaning is a profoundly creative act. It requires "thinking outside the box" when the box is constructed not just by what we *think*, by the knowledge and values that we have, but also by *how* we think, by our own habituated modes of reasoning.[1] The challenge is one that we all have faced: how to recognize the "box" when for all intents and purposes the "box" is determinative of what we experience as reality and is consequently invisible. Gadamer (2002) develops a foundation for engaging this box that is our mind, in his two-stage elaboration of the *hermeneutical circle*.

The *hermeneutical circle* refers to the logical dilemma that faces each person who reads a text. For clarity of this discussion, let's imagine that this text is a letter addressed to you, written in a foreign language, but translated into English. When you read the translated words, you begin to develop an understanding of what the writer was trying to say. Indeed, you anticipate the writer's meanings, projecting what was intended. However, some phrases seem ambiguous, and as you read, you realize that your interpretations and anticipations are not exactly what the writer seemed to mean. As you move through the letter, you constantly circle back to what was stated earlier, reconsidering the meanings you developed earlier with the new understanding you have gained. The *hermeneutical circle* is this paradoxical relation: you must read the parts to understand the whole, but you can't understand the parts until you've read the whole.

This circle ought to feel familiar. In conversations, we often fill in what people mean without hearing or understanding all of the words they say: inferring the whole from the words we comprehend; inferring the words we may not have heard from the meaning of the whole. But paradoxical or not, in this back-and-forth play between projected meanings and newly discovered meanings that require reconsideration of our projected meanings, we develop understanding of what the letter, or what our partner in dialogue, means.

---

[1] By modes of reasoning, we mean the different ways in which we create knowledge. This includes both the formal, disciplinary sorts of reasoning used to establish knowledge, such as mathematical reasoning, double-blind empirical reasoning in medicine, and ethical reasoning based upon reference to cultural or religious traditions. It also comprises informal modes of reasoning that individuals use to create their own knowledge. An individual's modes of reasoning may be eclectic amalgamations of various disciplinary forms and personalized patterns developed out of the individual's own socialization, life circumstances, and engagements with the world.

Our reference to a translated letter illustrates a further characteristic of importance in this constitutive dynamic. Knowing we are reading the words of a person socialized and writing from circumstances different than our immediate experience, we hold ourselves open to the possibility of new meanings, to the play of reconsideration. We expect that our initial projections of meaning may be wrong, and we expect to reconsider what we have understood. Herein is another important dynamic of dialogical understanding: our asserted meanings must always be held open to the further play of what the other means.

For Kenny, the raging student, and his teacher, the process of making sense of the events and their relation—the parts and the whole—is illustrative. First, the unacceptable behavior is explicitly described and a demand for action unequivocally stated, then the trigger events are recounted, then some history of previous events, then some glimpses into the mental frame of mind of both participants before the event, and then background circumstances that increased stressors on both and consequently decreased their capacity to foresee the trouble they were heading for and their capacity to find other alternatives. These ideas, and more, will certainly not emerge in a neat, sequential fashion; some emerge in the heat of an emotional exchange; others need to be encouraged, solicited, and extracted by the school principal dealing with the situation.

The principal's understanding grows as the parts of both participants' stories mesh and clash. Understanding grows further as she adds the observations of Kenny's classmates. The principal's "play" of initial projected meanings with her growing sense of the whole relationship shared by Kenny and the teacher, of which this incident is but a part, causes her to restrain from leaping to conclusions based upon the initial description of the unacceptable behavior.

Though we develop understanding with another through this play of projected meanings that are continuously being reconsidered in light of our advancing experience with another, Gadamer (2002) believed that this process by itself is still an insufficient description of how understanding occurs. Following an insight from Heidegger, Gadamer argued (p. 266) that one's own *prejudices* and situation influence strongly what and how one understands another in dialogue.

Being Situated

Every person brings to an encounter with a text or another person his or her own ideas—Gadamer calls them (2002) fore-conceptions, fore-meanings, and fore-structures—which influence significantly how a text or another person are understood. He argues that these preestablished "prejudices" constitute everything that we understand, not just what we know but how we know. Our prejudices are shaped by the tradition in which we are immersed from the moment of our birth. Gadamer intends the term *prejudices* to imply a much broader meaning than the purely negative connotation English speakers generally recognize. For Gadamer, prejudices determine the meanings that we find in a text or in another person's words. They are "conditions of understanding" (p. 277). A few examples will help jar us out of our expected meanings for this term. A fore-conception such as the Earth revolves around the sun is a prejudice. A fore-meaning such as murder is wrong is a prejudice. A fore-structure such as mathematical reasoning is also a prejudice. Thus, understanding without prejudices is impossible. What is helpful for us in both broadening our sense of the word prejudice and in applying this single term to such a wide variety of mental constructs is the resulting simplicity for expressing how our understanding is influenced by our own mental constructs, experiences, and modes of thought, no matter how valid or invalid those constructs may be.

The notion of prejudice is analogous to Bourdieu's notion of *habitus,* the series of built up dispositions that, over time, work to constitute our social and cultural contexts. Bourdieu suggests that habitus is "inculcated in childhood" and becomes "ingrained in the individual" to such an extent that it "functions as a powerful conservative force binding individuals to the social order" (Swingewood, 1998, p. 97). Habitus, moreover, comprises *fields* such as education, the church, the state, political parties—each with its own specific internal laws of logic, its own traditions and assumptions that help to shape our "prejudices."

Like Bourdieu, as a student of the history of ideas, Gadamer (2002) was very conscious of how a thinker's historical moment and geographical location, which Gadamer referred to as a person's situatedness, shaped his or her ideas. Yet, Gadamer is not willing to allow prejudices, inevitably present as they are, to remain unconscious. "It is the tyranny of hidden prejudices that makes us deaf to what speaks to us ..." (p. 270). To bring to the foreground these prejudices so that we may make conscious their effects on the meanings of others is a constant, difficult, never ending, but absolutely necessary task.

No matter how reflective the thinker, his or her thinking is always bounded by his or her situatedness. Gadamer (2002) writes:

> To acquire an awareness of a situation is, however, always a task of peculiar difficulty. The very idea of a situation means that we are not standing outside it and hence are unable to have any objective knowledge of it. We always find ourselves within a situation, and throwing light on it is a task that is never entirely finished. (p. 301)

To define our situation, we often begin with the intersection of the major sociological categories of race, class, gender, sexual orientation, and ability. But both Bourdieu and Gadamer would further insist on including the multitude of other factors present in any one person's situation as also having a bearing on one's meanings and one's understandings. Gadamer would have us include factors such as geographical location, family structures, immediate economic circumstances, the historical events that immediately precede and surround a person—global, national, provincial, local, personal—and all of the meanings that these factors hold for us. He insists on our recognizing the dynamic intersections of the multitude of factors that define our unique historical consciousness. Thus, when we understand a cross cultural text or another person, we are inextricably present. There is no objective position, no chance of removing ourselves from the moment of encounter with another. We must situate "the other meaning in relation to the whole of our own meanings or ourselves in relation to it" (Gadamer, 2002, p. 268).

Are we doomed then to living a life imprisoned in a hall of mirrors, merely understanding, and acting upon, distorted reflections of ourselves? Let's consider some prejudices and situational factors that, for the sake of illustration, one might bring to our raging student and teacher.

The principal (like all of us) brings to the situation her own experiences as a student, teacher, and principal. Imagine that she is enrolled in a graduate course in the sociology of education, extending her already strong liberal arts orientation. Her parenting experience inclines her to hear both sides of the story before making a decision. The teacher, situated differently, with a strong inclination to authoritative behaviors, structures, and expectations, is deeply committed to his pronouncement and has little time for discussion, much less the implied questioning of his judgment and authority. But you can imagine the principal applying her new graduate course knowledge and analyzing the sociological patterns and power relations of the situation. She observes that the male teacher is of the dominant culture, while the student is from a poor family and a minoritized community that is emerging from a history of oppression. Add to these "prejudices" that the principal had once been bullied by this teacher when she had been particularly vulnerable as a new principal and thus was suspicious of his use of his own power. And further, she has a visceral, reflexive response to his approach to this student due to her own childhood experience of a teacher who had lost his temper with her. Finally, the paper she had finished the previous night on social justice and student advocacy by administrators would give her well constructed words to argue her case. Of course, there will be other factors (prejudices) that will incline her approach and significantly influence her understanding and actions; we are all much more complex individuals than one can capture by listing a few characteristics or describing several background experiences. In this case, the principal's situatedness and prejudices bring her into conflict with the understandings and actions of both teacher and student.

The point is that we can never get away from ourselves in the process of understanding another. But this does not mean that we cannot understand another. To do so, we must make ourselves open to the other. We become open through an unflagging, self-conscious vigilance, making conscious our prejudices and situatedness as best we can. We become open through an unswerving commitment to seek understanding with the other. We become open through an unremitting commitment to understand the other's meanings in their significance for that person. We become open by asking genuine questions.

Being Vigilant

To be open to the other requires our conscious awareness of the presence and influence of our prejudices and situatedness. This includes those prejudices and those situational factors that we have made conscious and the acknowledgment that there are other prejudices and situational factors influencing our thinking of which we are not yet aware. In *The Fifth Discipline*, Peter Senge (1990) writes that for dialogue to occur, participants must "suspend assumptions" (p. 241). David Bohm (1996) on whose (then unpublished) theory and practical experience Senge based his understanding of dialogue, calls for people to learn the skill of suspending the judging process so that people who would participate in dialogue may hear others with clarity. This starts us in the right direction. Both Bohm and Senge are advocating the importance of self-awareness of one's thinking and a qualified pausing of one's train of thought, slowing or stopping its career down pre-laid tracks. However, their call to suspend assumptions does not recognize the degree to which one's understanding is shaped by prejudices and situatedness and consequently mistakes the difficulty and narrows the scope of awareness necessary for opening one's thinking to that of another. Furthermore, they ignore the presence of ongoing prejudices that do not disappear when one suspends a judgment or two. We remain situated in the *habitus* of our traditions and experience.

Thinking of dialogue as technique (as Senge's description appears to suggest) seems to promise a do-this-once-and-you're-done process, disguising the necessity of the back-and-forth play of meanings—between parts and whole, between one's own meanings and the other's meanings, sometimes over a long period of time. To become open to the meanings of another we must foreground our prejudices in their multiple forms and our situatedness, expecting in the back-and-forth play of meanings with the other to discover further "prejudices" of which we were unaware. We become open to understanding the meanings of another when we are vigilant.

Being Committed

We also become open to understanding through commitment. Although this would seem to go without saying, the consequence of making a commitment to dialogue is to commit to awareness of one's own meanings and commit to making available the necessary time, energy, and space to engage the meanings of the other person. Burbules (1993), as we saw in the previous chapter, identifies commitment as one of the three defining "rules" (or what we are calling guiding principles of dialogue); the other two are reciprocity and participation. He writes:

> Engagement in this type of communicative relation [dialogue] must allow the flow of conversation to be persistent and extensive across a range of shared concerns, even difficult or divisive ones. This principle also requires sufficient commitment to, and confidence in, the communicative process to be willing to disclose one's underlying reasons, feelings, and motivations, when asked. (p. 81)

By giving our attention to the other, we are pushing aside all other considerations and concerns (Noddings, 1992), aware that the topic which we are seeking to understand may be troublesome and exhausting.

In effect, to commit to understand another is analogically similar to creating "a third space" in which one's own meanings and those of others may be presented and considered (Burbules, November 2002, personal communication). In the busy, often exhausting life of an educational leader, holding open this third space is a particular challenge.

The term "third space" is intended to suggest the need for a "space"— physical, emotional, intellectual, or spiritual—in which, to some degree, people can come together unfettered by the constraints and structures of institutional life. Parker Palmer (1998) defines space in this way:

> By *space* I mean a complex of factors: the physical arrangement and feeling of the room, the conceptual framework that I build around the topic my students and I are exploring, the emotional ethos I hope to facilitate, and the ground rules that will guide our inquiry. The space that works best for me is one shaped by a series of paradoxes. (p. 73)

We put forward the need for a third space to metaphorically convey the importance of finding new ways to relate and understand one another within our institutions of schooling, a topic we take up again in Chapter 6.

Confirming the Other's Meaning

A commitment to understand requires a further dimension; namely, that one must be committed to understanding the other's meanings in their significance for the other. Much as starting with the Golden Rule must not mean starting with self, neither can understanding distort the meanings of other people, reshaping them to our own meanings. Gadamer (2002) writes, "working out appropriate projections, anticipatory in nature, to be confirmed 'by the things' themselves, is the constant task of understanding" (p. 267).

There are two interdependent aspects here that require elaboration. First, we should expect to elaborate meanings that are congruent with the person from whom they arise, whether or not they are consistent with our own. And second, the other should confirm for us that what we have understood is what he or she meant.

It is not enough just to create a third space. We must be willing to hear the other's meanings in their uniqueness, expect them to be different from our own meanings to some degree, and do the work necessary to discern those meanings. This is more than just repeating back the other's words. This calls for more than a weak analogy ("that reminds me of the time my aunt Edna ...") that merely overwrites the other's meanings with one's own story. But getting the right words and relating genuine analogies play an important role. When we genuinely struggle for words, using our own words ("When you said you just wanted to rip the test up, it sounds like you were very frustrated?"), and when we suggest authentic analogies ("What you say seems to be similar to what I experience when ..."), we are attempting to align our own language and its referents, and our own experiences, with the other's. We may even take on the physical posture of the other as he or she communicates his or her meanings. Again the concept of back-and-forth play is crucial because in our struggle for the right words and analogous experiences, we wait for the other to confirm our representations in their accuracy, or lack thereof.

The other validates our understanding, providing agreement that what we say is what he or she meant, disagreeing when we have not got things quite right. When the other responds to our words with a rebuttal or to our analogies with an affirming extension, we are able to refine our understanding further. Gadamer observes that in the process of seeking the right words, it is quite likely that a new constellation of meanings for words may be created. In effect, those engaged in dialogical understanding develop a new language for themselves. When they meet and take up their dialogue with each other, the words that they previously defined will remain as their established vocabulary. Gadamer writes,

> Every conversation presupposes a common language, or better, creates a common language. Something is placed in the center, as the Greeks say, which the partners in dialogue both share, and concerning which they can exchange ideas with one another. Hence reaching an understanding on the subject matter of a conversation necessarily means that a common language must first be worked out in the conversation. This is not an external matter of simply adjusting our tools; nor is it even right to say that the partners adapt themselves to one another but, rather, in a successful conversation they both come under the influence of the truth of the object and are thus bound to one another in a new community. (2002, p. 379)

Gadamer brings us to an important recognition of the nature of commitment that we have been exploring. This commitment to open a third space and to hear the meanings of the other as they are meant by the other is nothing less than a commitment to create together "a new community" (the topic to be further explored in Chapters 4–6).

Genuine Questioning

Posing a genuine question to another person is one way of being open to the meanings of another. A genuine question has the power to reveal the known world of the questioner, in all of his or her complexity and naïveté. Creating a genuine question comprises everything that the questioner understands of the topic at that moment. Such genuine questions often feel risky: we make ourselves vulnerable when we ask them. This is not only because we risk exposing our degree of ignorance (not a comfortable thing for a person in authority), but also because a genuine question opens a space of uncertainty. Gadamer writes:

> To ask a question means to bring into the open. The openness of what is in question consists in the fact that the answer is not settled. It must still be undetermined, awaiting a decisive answer.... The sense of every question is realized in passing through this state of indeterminacy, in which it becomes an open question. Every true question requires this openness. (2002, p. 363)

Sometimes, educators and educational leaders set questions for students and others when the answers are already known, be these answers physics facts or disciplinary outcomes. These are not genuine questions as we understand them, but rather rhetorical devices intended to move the other's thinking in a predetermined direction. The focus is on the answer, rather than the other person. These questions are monological and do not require meaningful engagement with another person. A genuine, dialogical question erupts from an unchecked realization that the questioner does not know and that he or she wants to know. Thus, the simple posing of an authentic question opens us to understanding another.

Simultaneously, a genuine question provides the other an opportunity to explore his or her own world, as revealed by the unique limits of the question, and reveal this world to the questioner in terms the questioner has put and may therefore understand.

When the principal asks the teacher and student, "Would you be willing to talk about this further?" she indicates her propensity for dialogue.

When either teacher or student responds, "We can try," there is both openness and risk—openness to a renewed process and possible relationship and risk that the other will reject the possibility. The risk one takes by authentically responding to the question matches the risk taken by the questioner. The questioner's openness invites an equally open response. Thus, the "play" of significations begins.

In summary, we make ourselves open to another by recognizing that our very engagement with the other is deeply and inextricably influenced by our prejudices and situatedness. We open our thinking when we are guided by the possibility that our unconscious prejudices and unrevealed situatedness will continue to influence what we understand and acknowledge that we must be prepared to take account of this. We open ourselves to understanding the other when we commit the effort of will to encounter the other and dedicate the resources necessary to open a third space between us, a space defined by commitments to hear the other in his or her difference and to await the other's confirmation of our understanding. We open ourselves to the other when we seek to align our words and experiences with the other, developing a new and common language that binds us in a community of shared meanings. We open ourselves to the other when we pose a genuine question, a question that erupts from the edge of our known world into the space of what it is we realize we do not know but wish to. When we are open to another and allow the play of significations to occur between us, understanding grows. Gadamer suggested a metaphor for illustrating this process: he called it the "fusion of horizons."

Fusion of Horizons: A Dialogue of Understanding

While from the bounded level of our mind
Short views we take, nor see the lengths behind;
But more advanc'd, behold with strange surprise
New distant scenes of endless science rise!
So pleas'd at first the tow'ring Alps we try,
Mount o'er the vales, and seem to tread the sky,
Th' eternal snows appear already past,
And the first clouds and mountains seem the last;
But, those attain'd, we tremble to survey
The growing labours of the lengthen'd way,
Th' increasing prospects tire our wandering eyes,
Hills peep o'er hills, and Alps on Alps arise.

Alexander Pope (1711), lines from *Essay on Criticism*

Gadamer's (2002) metaphor of the horizon and Pope's poetic depiction of it richly portray our knowing. Imagine, if you will, standing on a slight rise. You are surrounded by a complex landscape stretching to a distant horizon. You are a part of this landscape, the center of it. All of your thoughts, plans, and actions occur in this landscape. It holds enormous opportunities that you see as you turn and survey its breadth; yet, at the same time, there are limits—the horizon is always present.

Now consider that this landscape is constituted of your own experiences, your beliefs, your attitudes, your knowledge, your thinking processes, your emotional inclinations, your aspirations, your habits of action, your circumstances for action. On your hill you see your prejudices and situatedness spreading out before you, behind you, all around you, stretching to your horizon, which is, in fact, the limit not of yourself but of your consciousness of yourself and your surroundings. Now take an important imaginative leap: consider that this landscape is not your prejudices and situatedness about everything in life, but rather about one specific thing, one subject. You stand, your conscious awareness at the center of a complex landscape of prejudices and situatedness, focusing on any single topic you may consider: what constitutes a good education, your favorite food, upcoming contract negotiations, or perhaps your relationship with a particular student? Some of your knowledge is closer, more pressing, sharply detailed, harder to see beyond. At the edges of your awareness, other prejudices and situatedness come into view—harder to define, but still present.

Finally, you perceive the limit of this landscape. But even as you become aware of this horizon, you become aware of the possibility of a beyond. Now imagine how you might begin to communicate all that constitutes your horizon to another person such that he or she can begin to understand what you mean.

We all stand at the center of such a horizon with regard to any topic. Gadamer wants us to recognize that in the process of dialogical understanding, we are simultaneously engaging another who is similarly situated in an ever-expanding landscape of meaning. In dialogue, we are expanding our own horizon to include the other's meanings and discovering what they mean to us. The metaphor illustrates how new knowledge may move us from our center, beyond the limits of our old landscape, over the horizon into a new landscape. It equally suggests the possibility of new knowledge expanding our horizons, widening our perspective, enlarging the landscape that we bring to our understanding of a topic.

Much as is portrayed in Pope's poem, Gadamer proposed the metaphor as a means to show that our knowledge is *limited* but not *fixed*. Moving toward the new vistas expands your horizon to include what you once did not know. Your horizon extends as you move. Moreover, when he wrote, "understanding is always the fusion of these horizons supposedly existing by themselves" (p. 306), Gadamer wished to suggest that in dialogical understanding, the horizons of participants reach a point where their individual horizons are present to each other in some degree, where participants see the other's horizon within or perhaps beyond their own. This is not to say that either participant loses his identity in some sort of fusion of identities where differences are merged or submerged. Nor is it to say that perfect understanding is achieved and all that constitutes each individual's horizon is now subsumed into the other. But rather it is to say that in the process of developing understanding, the complex landscape constituted by our prejudices and situatedness is communicated and grasped in some measure within the complex landscape of the other, and visa versa. It helps to keep in mind that, as in Pope's poem, Gadamer's notion that the back-and-forth play of significations that brings about this "fusion of horizons" may be without end. Understanding others may never be fully accomplished because their horizons, too, are dynamic and ever expanding.

Metaphors are unruly things, opening up meanings not necessarily intended. Many commentators and critics of Gadamer's "fusion" metaphor have mistakenly assumed that "fusion" implied a loss of identity and a loss of difference. This was not Gadamer's intention and certainly is not ours. We turn to Bakhtin to help reign in "fusion's" connotations. Bakhtin (1973b, p. 71) says that in dialogue people meet at their borders:

> Human thought becomes genuine thought, i.e., an idea, only under the conditions of a living contact with another foreign thought, embodied in the voice of another person, that is, in the consciousness of another person as expressed in his word.

We may use the horizon metaphor in a similar fashion to indicate that persons in dialogue encounter each other's difference when they meet at their respective horizons. What both of these images reflect is empirically represented in Vygotsky's (1978) explanation of the "zone of proximal development"—that space of optimal learning that exists at the edge of one's experienced and understood world. In the zone of proximal development, as at one's borders or at one's horizon line, one stands within the circle of one's established truths and ventures beyond to create new knowledge, to develop new understandings.

As Pope suggested three centuries ago, no sooner do we believe we have reached the limit of our horizon, or begun to fuse our horizon with that of another, than we discover vast new horizons, previously unknown and certainly unexplored. Even as we reach out and begin to communicate, we become aware of more hills, further valleys, the limitless unknown with the potential to continuously modify, renew, and re-create understanding.

We have argued that in the process of dialogue, new knowledge is developed by all participants. This is to say that understanding occurs. Gadamer elaborates the important role of questioning and testing in this process of meaning making:

> To conduct a conversation means to allow oneself to be conducted by the subject matter to which the partners in the dialogue are oriented. It requires that one does not try to argue the other person down but that one really considers the weight of the other's opinion. Hence it is an art of testing. But the art of testing is the art of questioning. For we have seen that to question means to lay open, to place in the open. As against the fixity of opinions, questioning makes the object and all its possibilities fluid. A person skilled in the "art" of questioning is a person who can prevent questions from being suppressed by the dominant opinion. (2002, p. 367)

In a dialogue, the knowledge that is created will be about the object in question, as exemplified in Gadamer's example above; it is also knowledge about ourselves, as we reflect on the prejudices and situatedness that formed our opinions previously and that are changed, to some degree, in the process of understanding. It is about the other participants whose meanings, prejudices, and situatedness are equally revealed.

The dynamics that enable this new knowledge include a play of significations and an openness of mind that facilitate a fusion of horizons. These dynamics may be enacted in a multitude of ways; dialogue is not reducible to a prescription or a method, but rather is a process that uniquely evolves out of a desire to understand another's meanings. When we commit to such a process, we, the whole school, and the wider community, submit to the possibility of "being transformed into a communion in which we do not remain what we were" (Gadamer, 2002, p. 379).

The Value of Dialogical Understanding for Educational Leadership

In the second section of this book, we will consider in more detail the benefits and applications of dialogical understanding for educational leaders in school communities. In the remainder of this chapter, we will map out where the dynamics of dialogical understanding may lead and provide some practical reasons for the educational leader to seek dialogical understanding.

Educational leaders are immersed in social worlds. They describe their lives as political, caring, interactive, sometimes challenging, tense, confrontational, emotional, organizational, interpersonal, sometimes rewarding, and intensely personal. Mark remembers how on some days it seemed that each of the thousand students, two thousand parents, seventy-five staff, twenty district staff, forty-odd fellow administrators, hundreds of school neighbors, eight school board members, and indeterminate numbers of community members including media could decide that now was the time pull on the invisible but deeply plugged-in connection that bound him to each of them through his school administrator role. Your experiences, as are Carolyn's, are likely similar. Educational leaders do not accomplish their ends with hammers or tractors or mutual funds, but *with* and *through* people. Educational leaders seek ways to serve people and they achieve these goals through uniting the multiple talents of the people with whom they work into shared collective action. Dialogical understanding holds rich promise for the unique context and goals of educational leaders. This promise arises from the development of new knowledge, new modes of reasoning, and the potential for mutual action.

Developing New Knowledge

In the hurly-burly of human relations prevalent in a school or a school district, the need for generating new knowledge is a constant priority. What are our hopes for the children in our care for the next 12 years? What are their hopes? Their parents' aspirations? How shall we achieve these? Is the intermediate science curriculum adequately preparing students for scientific reasoning? Why is this new student failing to thrive in John's classroom? What is the best way to introduce new technologies into the school? The list of questions, of areas of engagement needing new knowledge, is endless. Such is the educational enterprise.

Through dialogical understanding, at least four sorts of "new knowledge" are created. These include:

- knowledge of the other's horizon on a subject and knowledge of the other as revealed in encountering this specific horizon
- knowledge that the other gains of your horizon on a subject and knowledge of you as revealed in encountering this specific horizon
- knowledge that results from the synthesis of these two horizons
- knowledge that one gains regarding one's own horizon—one's prejudices and situatedness—as well as working out one's own meanings more completely.

Let's consider each in turn. New knowledge of the other's horizon on a subject and new knowledge of a subject provides a basis for understanding differently. If it is a high school timetable that is under consideration, then the perspective of an art teacher who prefers longer class times may be a valued perspective for opening up a wider discussion on how class time affects student learning in specific areas. This knowledge also provides a basis for understanding the other's perspective on the subject. Knowledge of the other developed through dialogical understanding permits one to experience the other's talents, modes of thinking, and ways of communicating. Knowing that the art teacher feels very strongly about changing the timetable to enable longer class time is important. The creative and convincing manner in which the art teacher made her position understood is valuable for an educational leader to know when it comes time to select a spokesperson on the subject. This new knowledge generated with, and about, the art teacher also has the potential to expand the number of topics about which the educational leader and the art teacher may further dialogue in the future. New knowledge creates the opportunity for further knowledge development.

New knowledge of the other's horizon on a subject and of the other gained through dialogical understanding is particularly relevant when modes of reasoning differ. This is the case when participants in the dialogue may come from different cultures, classes, or religions or have different sexual orientations (to name only a few possibilities) and may emphasize significant epistemological, ontological, or teleological differences. It is also the case that such differences are often politically charged. In these situations, dialogical understanding can permit an educational leader to begin to reason as the other reasons, to see his or her horizons, and hence to consider her or his own thoughts, decisions, and actions from the other's point of view. When this kind of understanding occurs, what constitutes important knowledge for all participants is more likely to be anticipated, created, and legitimated.

If it is valuable for an educational leader to develop new knowledge with regard to a member of her or his learning community, it is equally valuable for others to develop new knowledge of the educational leader. The art teacher may learn that there are also negative consequences for extended class periods in other programs in the school. The educational leader benefits when the art teacher understands the balancing of different needs essential to a constructive assessment of a new timetable. The art teacher may also learn that the educational leader does not have a fixed position with regard to the timetable or that she does not automatically "side with" the science department's perspective—important realizations that may dispel a sense of futility and cynicism around the discussion.

Finally, the art teacher may learn that the educational leader, although not promising to enact the art teacher's wishes, nevertheless listened carefully and understood more fully what the art teacher's aspirations were. Learning this about the educational leader may open up the possibility of exploring other topics that until then the art teacher had buried. Understanding of the educational leader by others is vital for successful leadership to occur. From such understanding, others may position themselves in relation to the educational leader with some degree of certainty that the educational leader will respond in a predictable fashion. Upon such security, new directions may be risked, issues clearly expressed, and new plans developed.

The fusion of horizons between an educational leader and others around a specific topic potentially generates a completely different set of possibilities than were evident to any of the participants before this synthesis of perspectives occurred. In the case of the high school timetable, a synthesis of perspectives might result in a compromise structure in which there are days when blocks are short and days when blocks are doubled in length or in which there are longer morning classes and shorter afternoon sessions. Or a synthesis may suggest that there are benefits to organizing students into a semester of long studio-type courses to be followed by a semester of courses that require short periods. Or perhaps the district as a whole takes on the issue by recognizing the different requirements of students dedicated to various learning programs and setting up one school with an emphasis on those courses that benefit from long block scheduling and another with an emphasis on those courses that benefit from short block scheduling. In the course of exploring the horizons of all participants, the seeds of a completely new direction may be present, though invisible to all until each understands the other. Significantly, this synthesis does not just imply knowledge being combined to form different alternatives, but potentially new modes of reasoning that create knowledge unlike any knowledge brought to the table by participants. From such processes, new educational visions are born.

Knowledge one gains about one's own meanings, situatedness, and motivations and about one's own horizon is fundamentally valuable to an educational leader. Often when we engage in dialogue with another, we do not have a clear sense of what we think or mean about a subject. Indeed, we may search out others as sounding boards just to hear how an idea sounds. In the process of dialogue, the other's questions and our own answers open up to our awareness meanings that were hidden or only half-formed. Sometimes, the other's questions sharpen our meanings, testing them, as Gadamer said, such that we become confident that they are internally coherent. Equally, in dialogue when we engage the horizon of another, our own horizon of prejudices and situatedness may become clearer in the encounter. The other facilitates our own foregrounding of that knowledge and those modes of reasoning which are active in our horizon but of which we are not yet aware. Being more aware, we have the potential to become more open to the subject and to the other(s) that we engage. Better moral, ethical, and more purposeful leadership may result.

Engaging in Mutual Action

Dialogical understanding enables mutual action even in situations where significant differences make action difficult, perhaps especially in situations where significant differences make action difficult. There are several reasons for this. First, dialogue provides opportunities to develop relationships with others, relationships that overcome the lack of awareness which may inhibit trust and the possibility of risking action. Second, dialogical understanding by virtue of its back-and-forth dynamic results in a collaborative knowledge-producing process that, in itself, is a pattern for deliberating together, deciding together, acting together, and reflecting on action together. Third, dialogical understanding never presumes to speak for the other, but always holds itself open to a further response from the other (as both Bakhtin and Gadamer say, dialogue is never finished). Fourth, as dialogical understanding of a subject deepens and the range of subjects about which participants may dialogue widens, participants in dialogue increasingly can anticipate each other's reasoning processes, each other's intentions, each other's aspirations (we are familiar with situations in which we can predict the other's gesture or turn of phrase or in which we can accurately even "finish the thought" of the one with whom we interact). The capacity to expect the other's modes of reasoning, values, and aspirations increases the comfort of the relationship.

Although one must always be cautious not to assume too much, having had the opportunity to understand the other's perspective increases trust and, therefore, the ability to act together. Such certainty is crucial for integrated collective action. Moreover, as mutual understanding of respective horizons deepens, the depth of engagement by participants also deepens. Risk taking increases. Moving from the ground of certain knowledge to areas of uncertainty shifts participants beyond habituated truths and positional posturing into the creative ambiguity of possibilities and aspirations.

How the raging teacher and student finally came to terms with each other, in this true situation, is illustrative. They each took the risk of engaging in a dialogic relation that might resolve the situation. They both described the sorts of restitution necessary from the other to reestablish their relationship on respectful terms. Conversations that followed this restitution were very productive. Both agreed that the learning environment was not working for either. The student was temporarily removed from the class. But both teacher and student continued to work on the relationship and to build understanding. They decided to try working in one-on-one situations. During class time, Kenny worked independently in the library, but he checked with the teacher daily before school started for 15 minutes. They developed a deeper understanding of each other. Eventually the student returned to class. The next semester, the student enrolled with the teacher for an elective and did very well.

Dialogical understanding developed among the participants a shared set of meanings and a shared language that made the communicative foundation of collective action possible. The ability to join with another in communion does not mean a loss of identity or an ignoring of difference, but rather requires a joining together around a shared understanding, new to both, which permits common action as allies. The new working relationships between Kenny and his teacher are examples of fresh, shared understandings.

Educational leaders who participate in dialogical understanding and facilitate its dynamics throughout an educational community will serve parents, students, and teachers in new ways. They will achieve educational aspirations through the synergy of many people's different knowledge, modes of reasoning, talents, and commitment. Such is the promise of dialogical understanding.

PART TWO

Dialogue as Builder and Boundary Breaker

"Hopeful High School" is a medium-size, multiethnic school located in a mixed, but relatively low socio-economic area of a large urban center. By reputation, the school is a challenging, but cheerful, focused, caring, and affirming place to work. Teachers posted there are envied by their peers. Students are enthusiastic about learning, involved in extracurricular activities, leadership, and community service. They show up for class with their homework done, papers prepared, and eyes alert, hungry for the interaction that occurs in each classroom. They debate, argue, question, and converse as they work in small groups on meaningful projects. Sometimes they work alone, delving deeply into a topic of great personal interest. The parents proudly visit classes to see their children present their latest idea or project; they volunteer to assist with school activities or to share their knowledge. Disciplinary incidents are so rare that the vice-principal can hardly ever be found in her office dealing with unruly students, but rather in gathering places, interacting with students.

Teachers and school administrators have received many kudos from their district office; they are often invited to speak at conferences and professional development activities. These are the occasions when, as a team, they share how they have gotten to know something about the life of each student outside of school, how, having tried all of the new programs and best practices available to no avail, they opted for a radical new focus. As educators, they took responsibility for the quality of life in the school, for positive interactions, respectful relationships, meaningful curriculum, and inclusive pedagogy. The difference is amazing and yet, they do not seem to be working harder than their colleagues in less successful schools. Hopeful High School is a joyful, caring, high-achieving school—one with which they are proud to be associated.

When asked how they could possibly have turned around a school that was so diverse, with so many children coming from financially impoverished situations and so many people for whom English is a second language, they smile. "We began to take responsibility," they say, "not just for teaching the curriculum, but for teaching the children. We stopped blaming outside forces beyond our control (the parents, the system, the teacher from last year who really could not have done her job responsibly). We got to know them, built relationships, and developed understanding."

***

Hopeful High School, like its counterpart, Hopeless High School of Part One, is mythic. It does not exist in the pure form in which it is presented here. If Hopeless High is the shadow side of Any High, then Hopeful High is its light counterpart—the side that comes into play when respect and inclusion are found, when students are engaged in meaningful learning, and when the community believes it is attaining its goals. As for Hopeless High, there are elements of Hopeful High in almost every school we know. Sometimes, it is true, the characteristics of hopefulness and evidences of "success" seem few and far between. Sometimes they are buried by the mountains of paperwork and the morass of problems that seem to confront educators on a daily basis. But, hopefulness can be found wherever teachers form positive relationships with their students, where they understand that opportunity to learn is as critical as ability to learn, and where educators focus on creating spaces and opportunities for students to make connections between and among each other and between their curricular content and their daily lives. Indeed, we believe that the successes of Hopeful High School occur as educators take seriously the need for creating a sense of community within their schools as they engage in the dialogue that permits community to flourish.

In the previous chapters, we focused on why we think dialogue is sorely needed. We presented an image of dialogue built upon relationship and understanding. And we emphasized strongly that dialogue is not just talk, not just another communication strategy, but that dialogue is actually the gift of life lived fully and abundantly with others.

To this point, we have focused on dialogue as interaction primarily between two people. We have met Mrs. Davis, several school principals, a teacher, Kenny, and Sonny—all have helped us to develop a model of dialogue in which relationships and understanding are fundamental to our being, in which dialogue stands in the center as the means to enhance relationships, achieve understanding (if always partial), and live in openness to other human beings. We have acknowledged the spiraling nature of dialogue: as we increase understanding, relationships deepen; as relationships deepen, we become open to new understandings and insights. We have found, paradoxically, that although trust and liking are not pre-requisite to dialogue, as relationships and understanding expand and intensify, so, too, do trust, affection, and caring increase. We have noted Burbules' (1993) guiding principles that dialogue requires participation, commitment, and reciprocity.

Thus, we have developed a concept of dialogue as the cornerstone of individual relations, but it is also the building block for communal relations in schools, and it is to this latter topic to which we now turn our attention. We are well aware that the one-to-one interactions we have described to this point do not encompass many of the exchanges that occur in schools. Teacher-leaders are confronted on a daily and hourly basis with classes comprised of many individual students. Sometimes dialogue occurs with one person, sometimes it occurs with a small group, at times it occurs among students without a teacher's intervention, and on rare occasions, dialogue may occur with the whole class at once. For school administrative leaders, dialogic interaction occurs both formally and informally: in the halls, in the staffroom, at a sporting event, as well as at formal meetings, large and small.

In the next three chapters, we take the dialogical foundation we have developed and demonstrate how it forms the basis for creating community—community that has its roots in multiple, individual dialogic relations, embedded in wider socio-cultural contexts. We believe that the lessons learned in the first section provide insights into how educational leaders may encourage, facilitate, model, and engage dialogue in multiple sites, on various occasions, and at numerous times throughout the day. And we believe that as we multiply the occurrences of dialogue within a school, the collective will become a community—one that draws its wisdom, strength, and power from renewed relationships and deeper understandings.

We have already demonstrated that without respect or absolute regard for the other as intrinsically worthy of being understood, there can be no dialogue. We have also established that meaningful understanding occurs when we acknowledge our prejudices and situatedness and, in openness to another, achieve a sort of fusing of horizons. We have laid the basis for deeply democratic school communities, grounded on respect, understanding, and relationship, increasing in trust and affection, and consciously choosing dialogue as the foundation of the community.

We have come to believe that when educational leaders have the competencies and capacity for, and commitment to, the centrality of dialogue, they find in it the impetus and resources for the development of inclusive, democratic, and excellent school communities. They understand the potential of dialogue to transform our systems and structures of education as the dialogue whirls, gyrates, and spirals, creating complex and perpetually changing interactions of relationship and understanding.

In Chapter Four, we provide an overview of some ways of thinking about dialogue in community, criteria, if you like, for examining, reflecting on, and assessing our progress toward a new form of transformative leadership that is grounded in dialogue and that takes account of power relations (for good and ill) in a school community. In Chapter Five, we expand our concept of dialogue to demonstrate how it can offer hope and guidance not just for relationships and understanding between two people, but to those wanting to create school communities in which adults and children alike experience social justice and achieve academic excellence. Dialogue is central to the understanding of deeply democratic community, sometimes known as a *community of difference* (Furman, 1998; Murthada-Watts, 1999; Shields & Seltzer, 1997), that we develop here. (However, once again, we acknowledge that dialogue is a necessary but not sufficient condition of community.)

Chapter Six takes us further by helping us to think about the ways in which, when we appear to have reached a stalemate in our attempts to foster dialogue and create deeply democratic community, we may actually break the barriers and move forward. There we introduce the concepts of *carnival* and *play* as central to overcoming institutional barriers and instituting dialogic community. We demonstrate that when we find ways to break out of our current ways of thinking, to free ourselves from our established structures and cultures of schooling, we also find ways to empower each other as players in the dynamic and exciting life game of being together in the world. Dialogic relations and understandings provide the basis for this game.

We hope that as you join us in the move from individual I-Thou relations, engage in the to-and-fro play of understanding and their compelling connections and insights, and move to a focus on communal interactions, you will be gripped, as we are, by a sense of the importance and power of dialogic leadership for the transformation of our schools.

CHAPTER FOUR

Dialogue in Community Settings

Mosaic Community School is a two-story, painted brick building, situated in the cement heart of a large urban area. It comprises 450 students who speak 27 different languages in their homes and come from multiple ethnic and cultural backgrounds. The transiency rate in the school exceeds 100% annually. Many children live in poverty; many parents hold several jobs, striving for a better life for themselves and their children; many live in substandard housing. Many parents speak little English, have little formal education, and communicate rarely with the school. Others, however, are well established and well educated. All care deeply about the welfare of their children.

In response to the needs of its students and the surrounding community, the school has developed an extensive list of programs: there is a community garden, a parent skills training program, a clothing exchange, a cooking and meals program, special Aboriginal program, and numerous programs of academic assistance. Among the latter are early childhood programs, itinerant learning assistance, pull-out learning assistance, an enrichment teacher, and a special class for children with "low incidence" learning needs. There are so many adults in the building that, including teachers, there is roughly a four-to-one student-adult ratio. The school benefits from the services of a neighborhood assistant, a multi-

cultural worker, a counselor, an Aboriginal support worker, several youth and family workers, and a librarian. Part-time assistants include a psychologist, a nurse, a speech and language pathologist, a police liaison officer, and a meal coordinator. Volunteers read to the children, assist with meal preparation, provide supplemental music lessons, and help in the library, office, and classrooms as required.

When we first entered the school, it gave the impression of a warm and vibrant community center: parents were sitting on the heavy, upholstered couches in the main foyer with their preschool children playing with toys scattered in abundance. We were amazed by the colorful art work on the walls, art that represented many of the communities from which the children came, some of it done by the students themselves.

There was a buzz about the place that, we learned, masked many of the deep-seated problems encountered both by the school and by individual families and children. The school had made an excellent start, but still too many children were failing to thrive academically. Too many students dropped out of high school before graduation; too many became involved in street gangs and fighting. Too many parents returned to their impoverished homes, lonely and in despair. Too many teachers were burning out, frustrated that they rarely had the opportunity to have all of their assigned students together because of the intervention of the support and assistance programs. Too many children were achieving far below grade level on recognized measures of academic performance.

We heard the suggestion frequently from staff and teachers: "We need to create a program to ensure that every child has one meaningful relationship with a caring adult every day!" With so many adults already in the building, so much effort, and so much good will, what was going wrong?

***

Mosaic Community School is not fictitious. Although we have provided it with a pseudonym, the school itself is one in which we have spent a considerable amount of time. It is, moreover, not unique, but resembles many other schools with which we are acquainted—schools in which educators are trying their best to make a difference in the lives of children, but feeling increasingly frustrated and burned out.

We believe that dialogue, with its dual emphasis on building relationships and creating understanding, may be the missing piece at Mosaic Community School and numerous schools like it that are trying to address the increasing diversity of their student populations with varying degrees of success and disappointment. We also believe that if the educational leaders could take a step back and assess their school using some benchmark criteria related to their goals, they would begin to identify areas in which dialogue is necessary and ways in which they might move forward by facilitating dialogical interactions. Hence, in this chapter, we want to introduce the concept of criteria for guiding dialogue and for assessing the impact of dialogue and the nature of the school communities in which we live and work. We also want to address the thorny issues of power that often seem to intervene to impede the forging of meaningful relationships and deeper understanding. These concepts will lay the groundwork for our discussions relating more fully, in Chapters Five and Six, to dialogue as the basis for both the creation and the re-creation of positive, powerful, and empowering educational communities.

Here, we hope to show how dialogue, when it is conceptualized in conjunction with criteria for social justice and academic excellence and when it includes careful consideration of the nature of power relations, might help us turn a turbulent school like Mosaic Community School into one that is deeply and joyfully democratic.

Criteria as a Basis for Dialogue

If we are to focus on the development of more healthy relationships, deeper understanding, and more inclusive and democratic communities, it behooves us as educational leaders to understand and be able to articulate what drives us, what moral purposes we are attempting to accomplish, and what criteria we have put in place to assess our progress.

We remind the reader that the notion of moral purpose as an integral, even essential, part of educational leadership, while not absolutely new, has only recently reemerged as an important focus. With the previous century's particular emphasis on efficiency and scientific management, moral purpose was often dismissed as soft and unmeasurable, as unworthy of a truly rational and scientific leader. Yet, in recent years, a long list of prominent educators has taken up the cause. Sergiovanni (1996), for instance, has argued for the need for an educational leader to "establish a moral voice." He writes:

> As simple as the idea of a moral voice is, it has the potential to revolutionize school leadership.... Community members are bonded together as they are bound to share commitments in a covenantal relationship.... If a secret exists that accounts for the power of community, it is the moral voice that community provides. (pp. 58–59)

Community, we argue, is critical to the success of what goes on in a school. Moreover, community, while based on relationships and understanding, must also be grounded in a sense of moral purpose, and the members of a community must learn to speak together with moral voices.

Barth (1990), in *Improving Schools from Within*, wrote about building a community of learners. He noted that "communities of learners seem to be committed above all to discovering conditions that elicit and support human learning and to providing these conditions" (p. 45). We have suggested that dialogue that creates relationships and enhances understanding is fundamental to supporting human learning. And while we have argued that everyone must be free to participate in the dialogue, that each person must be treated within a dialogic community with "absolute regard," we also believe that the nature of the dialogue itself is important.

Ira Bogotch (2000) has recently defined education as a "deliberate intervention that requires the moral use of power" (p. 2). This definition introduces the problematic topic of power, but combines it with the notion of action and moral purpose, here described as deliberate intervention. We acknowledge that achieving a fully inclusive, respectful, and democratic community or attaining social justice are ideals, moral purposes toward which educators strive. Likewise, dialogic leadership is an ideal; it is not a "thing" or "specific structure" to be reified, defined, reduced, observed, and replicated. Rather, dialogic leadership may be understood more usefully as a process or a way of "ethical living" (Maxcy, 1995) in a diverse society.

This is easy to say, but more difficult to accomplish; and for that reason, we have found it useful to consider criteria against which the school leader may assess his or her leadership. Kincheloe and Steinberg (1995), in the introduction to their book *Thirteen Questions*, state that systems of meaning that help us identify what type of schools we want to create or how we decide what we need to know, should be "just, democratic, empathetic,[1] and

---

[1]   As previously indicated, we use the authors' term *empathetic* when we cite them, but

optimistic" (p. 2). These four concepts provide a useful framework for assessing progress toward the multiple educational goals we are called to achieve in public schools. While others may choose alternate criteria against which to assess change, we find that these four provide excellent lenses through which to examine our relationships, our understandings, and our dialogue. But they must be considered carefully and holistically.

Justice

Justice requires us to examine what we mean by equity and equality. We once visited a comprehensive high school with a diverse student body. It offered a myriad of programs: vocational opportunities, regular academic classes, learning assistance, and English as a second language, enriched, advanced, gifted and talented, and International Baccalaureate classes. We noted, with surprise, that few young people aside from Chinese and Caucasian students occupied seats in the more academically challenging classes, and we began to inquire: Do you make any attempt to have proportional representation in your programs? Do you attempt to attract Aboriginal students to your gifted program? Have you ever had Aboriginal students in your International Baccalaureat or gifted classes?

Repeatedly we were told that all programs are open to all students but that some just choose not to apply. We wondered aloud whether students from underrepresented groups were invited or encouraged and were told they were not. We raised questions about whether entrance criteria for some programs might discriminate against some students or predispose others to believe they did not have the intellectual ability to participate. Finally, we were informed, "We had one Aboriginal student in the gifted program once, but she only lasted until October. We never did figure out why." We left, feeling concerned about the lack of dialogue that our questions had prompted and the apparent lack of openness to new ways of thinking about their programs.

If we accept the dimensions of equality posited by Farrell (1999)—access, survivability (sustainability), outputs, and outcomes—we will have a basis for entering into a dialogue about our school programs and allocation of resources. If students do not believe that particular programs are open to

---

prefer to use the more readily accepted and generally used term *empathic* for our own use.

them, whether they are technically "open" or not, one cannot claim equity of access. If the only Indigenous student drops out in October, there is certainly not equality of retention or survivability. When certain minoritized groups of students are de facto consigned to lower-level classes that lead to a more restricted set of future options, neither the outputs (their school performance) nor the outcomes (their postsecondary opportunities and achievements) may be considered just.

Hence, the justice criteria would provide a basis for some of the dialogue a leader might want to introduce in a school; they would lead the educational leader to ask numerous questions about the marketing of, recruitment to, and support for various school programs. What do members of various subgroups in the school understand about the intended goals of each program, about the purposes (moral or otherwise) that each is intended to achieve? How can we ensure just assignment of students (and teachers) to classes and just allocation of resources (fiscal, space, time, material) to programs? Who has participated in decisions about the community garden at Mosaic Community School? Who has been involved in the cooking classes? Who volunteers to hear the children read? Whose voices have always been heard? Who has been silent? How can we invite them into the dialogue? With whom should these topics be raised in order to enhance relationships and deepen understanding?

Democracy

We have advocated that schools should be deeply democratic. Although we have not defined the term, Green's explanation resonates with us. Democracy is a concept that "expresses the experience-based possibility of more equal, respectful, and mutually beneficial ways of community life ..." (1999, p. vi). We argue that to develop more equal, respectful, and mutually beneficial approaches to education, we need to enhance relationships and understanding by encouraging the participation of all members of the school community. To accomplish this requires overcoming (at least on a temporary basis) differences of status and power, surmounting the roles and responsibilities we have been assigned in institutional life, and treating the other with "absolute regard." When we apply the criterion of democracy, it is not sufficient to determine whether we have issued an inclusive invitation for a particular event, whether we have permitted adequate time at a meeting for the exploration of a specific topic, or even whether we have translated a newsletter or policy document into some of the dominant home languages spoken in our school community. We are obliged to consider whether barriers still remain to the full and equal participation of all members of the community. Have we discussed a new discipline policy among teachers without including students? Have we addressed the "failing Aboriginal student" problem without inviting the local Indigenous community to meet with us, on their terms, to tell us about their understanding of the issues and their relationships with the school? Have we made assumptions about what others know or want to know, assumptions that erect barriers to their participation?

We recall, with some embarrassment, the times when we (and other educational leaders whom we know) encouraged teachers to telephone parents to set up interviews with them during upcoming "parent–teacher conferences." Did we start by ensuring that each parent knew and understood the format and concept of a parent–teacher conference? Did they know whether their student was to accompany them or not? What about younger children— would there be provision for them? Were they expected to "know" anything or to "say" anything? How should they dress? What were the stakes for their child if they came and "made a mistake"? Might it be better if they simply did not show up? We made assumptions that parents, even those who spoke limited English, would ask us if they did not understand, would know intuitively what was expected, or could deduce the norms by watching others. We did not create the conditions under which we could engage in dialogue with many parents; indeed, we were not open to dialogue. We invited them and assumed that the invitation alone demonstrated caring, but we did not treat them with "absolute regard." There was no attempt on our part to start with their concerns, their needs, and their perceptions and to be open to them with our whole being.

In Mosaic Community School, educators also failed to engage parents and members of the community in discussions about their hopes for their children, ways in which they could work in partnership to achieve their dreams, or ways in which the school could better help them to meet the challenges of their daily lives. The educators were burning out, in part, because they had failed to act democratically. The school, although vibrant, was not inclusive. The educators had taken so much responsibility for *doing for* the parents and students, they had forgotten the power of *doing with*—of developing relationships with the parents, support workers, and students; of developing shared understandings of their aspirations and needs and how to address them; and of acting collectively to attain their goals.

The criterion of democracy requires not only that we invite people to participate, but that, in large part through dialogue, we create the conditions that actually enable their full participation. When dialogue is missing, deep democracy cannot be found.

Empathy and Caring

Kincheloe and Steinberg (1995) state that one meaning we should be able to identify in the kind of schools we desire is empathy. According to *Stedman's Online Medical Dictionary*, empathy is:

> The ability to intellectually and emotionally sense the emotions, feelings, and reactions that another person is experiencing and to effectively *communicate that understanding* to the individual. (our emphasis)

In the ability to communicate our understanding to others, we hear echoes of Gadamer's concept of to-and-fro play.

Another source, the *On-line Medical Dictionary*, states that empathy "includes caring, which is the *demonstration* of an awareness of and a concern for the good of others." Other dictionaries clearly differentiate between empathy and sympathy. For example, *Dorland's Illustrated Medical Dictionary* contains the following entry:

> empathy (em·pa·thy) (em′p[schwa]-the) [Gr. *en* into + *-pathy*] intellectual and emotional awareness and understanding of another person's thoughts, feelings, and behavior, even those that are distressing and disturbing. *Empathy* emphasizes understanding, *sympathy* emphasizes sharing, of another person's feelings and experiences.

We are attracted to these definitions in that they combine the intellectual and emotional, or cognitive and relational, aspects of relating to another that are at the heart of dialogue. Noddings (1992) has used the term *care* to convey similar meanings. She emphasizes that "caring is a way of being in relation, not a set of specific behaviors" (p. 17). Caring is not something we do, but what we are. Noddings' concept of care bears little resemblance to the ways in which care is sometimes thought about in schools as making students "feel good." Care is not a soft, fuzzy, and nebulous quality antithetical to rigorous intellectual inquiry; indeed, care is not anti-intellectual, but a pedagogical approach that takes into consideration the interests, aspirations, and aptitudes of the learner. Thus, it is care that permits us to respond "differentially" to our students.

The criterion of empathy reminds us that when we hold the other (child or adult) in absolute regard, we begin by trying to understand his or her position. But empathy requires more. Approaching the concept of empathy as it is sometimes used in art illustrates this point well. Argan (1955), biographer of the early Renaissance painter Fra Angelico, quotes him: "He who wishes to paint Christ's story must live with Christ." Here the notion of "living with" is interesting. It is not the sympathetic sharing of one's feelings and experiences, but rather a knowing about the other's situation—a fusing of the horizons Gadamer might say. A later German Expressionist painter, Emil Nolde, said of those whom he painted, "Occasionally, I feel that spiritually I participate in all these kinds of lives" (Nolde, 1934).

As a criterion for educational leaders, empathy requires us to examine what we call caring, to ensure that we are not going through a set of motions or even using a particular set of words, but that we are actually participating in—understanding—the situations of our students. This understanding must be different from the misplaced activities of some school counselors who seem to bury themselves in their students' feelings and situations, identifying so closely that they become ineffectual, losing sight of their role and of what is really in the best interests of the student. Understanding others (as we developed the concept in Chapter Three) and relating (as developed in Chapter Two) to others and to the hurts, fears, joys, and successes of those with whom we work permits dialogue to occur.

Living with, participating in—these are fundamental ways of being in community if we are to develop the types of empathic relationships and understandings we have been describing. When we live *with* teachers, parents, and students, they will know they are cared for and cared about. When we participate in their lives, we demonstrate our commitment to care. We develop the relationships that demonstrate that we care. And from these relationships grows the new and deeper understanding that closes the hermeneutic circle. Without relationship and understanding, we cannot foster the empathy required for the sustenance of our educational communities.

Optimism

Optimism sometimes has a bad name. Voltaire's (1759) *Candide*, who went around saying that "all things work for the best in the best of all possible worlds" despite encountering one tragedy after another, is the epitome of why we sometimes dismiss optimism as unrealistic, as putting the best face on a situation regardless of the reality. This is certainly not the optimism that we desire for educators and our systems of education. Our children deserve a more robust optimism, one that focuses on opening doors of opportunity and windows of understanding for all children—not just those who come to school with the most advantages.

The concept of optimism that we posit as a criterion for educational communities, communities that are deeply democratic and socially just, is quite different. It is akin to the Christian notion of hope—not as wishful thinking, but as "sure hope," a bedrock conviction that what we are involved in will have the desired outcomes for our students: outcomes that are socially just and academically excellent, outcomes that are grounded both in relationships and discernment. Optimism is also akin to Liston's (2001) concept of joy, a metaphor that helps "us understand, experience, and appreciate ideas and concepts that have not been previously thought to relate" (p. 2). Liston grounds her work in Buber's I-Thou relations and uses the concept as a way of *being* both aesthetically and ethically or

> as a reminder of our "call to care." Joy is compassionate and full of the possibilities of life. Joy rejects hierarchy and oppression and offers a world of fulfilment and justice. Joy brings our attention to the interrelatedness of each of us to each other of us. (p. 21)

Optimism and joy are the qualities we desire for Mosaic Community School. There, educators not only want, but need, to ensure opportunities for the students who seem most likely to participate in gang activities or to drop out of school when they are 16 to become connected to positive peer groups and adult role models. In other words, they need caring, supportive relationships. We not only want, but need, to ensure that the students who have the least home advantages are prepared academically and socially to succeed in whatever their chosen career path might be. We need to find ways to engage others in dialogue about what such opportunities and success might look like and how we might help the students and their families to achieve it.

Optimism draws together the concepts of justice, democracy, and empathy that have previously been developed. It is grounded in joyous and joyful relations with others—relations that open to them the possibilities of fulfilment, of opportunities, and of understanding. Taken together, these criteria provide various ways of thinking about school communities, multiple lenses for assessing our praxis, and a myriad of entry points for dialogue. Once enjoined, this dialogue will permit us to understand how we can help, but also the ways in which our "assistance" might be seen as patronizing, controlling, or hegemonic, as *doing for* in detrimental ways instead of *doing with* in dialogic relations. Freire (2000c) states that "if we want to work *with* the people and not just *for* them we have to know their game" (p. 259). In other words, we must understand others, their meanings, and their contexts, and we must take careful account of the nature of power relations which are omnipresent in all interactions, including dialogic interactions. Freire goes further. He asserts that he will always view in a good light ...

> relationships of mutual respect, dialogical relationships, through which we can grow together, learn together. On the contrary, I will always see negatively any so-called organization "of cooperation," which distortedly, however, intends to impose its options onto us in the name of the help it might give us. (p. 236)

Power, when it is misused, even with the intent of trying to help—perhaps especially with that intent, distorts and destroys the possibility of relationship as it denies the possibility of mutual regard.

When Dialogue Encounters Power

Much is made in both postmodern and critical educational writing of the notion of power and how power inequities and power hierarchies may constrain justice, prevent dialogue, inhibit participation, hinder communication, and oppose the attainment of justice and excellence. Here, we briefly examine the notion of power as it relates to our elaboration of dialogue as central to being, to understanding, and to relationships. We now address how power may work to constrain the potential of dialogue and then, in the last section of this chapter, focus on how we may, at least for a short time, "bracket" some of the constructs of power that exist in schools and engage in activities that facilitate dialogue by creating conditions that mitigate power relations and permit more equal community participation.

Michel Foucault provides some useful tools for conceptualizing power in institutional settings; hence, we draw on his work, although, as ever, the perspectives of other theorists also contribute to the *heteroglossia* and the *polyphony*—the multiple voices and perspectives—of this discussion. From Foucault's work we will consider two concepts of power that are relevant to any discussion of dialogical educational leadership. Central to his work is understanding how techniques of power turn individuals into subjugated "its." Second, we examine the concept of power as it relates to the *situatedness* (to use the term we have previously identified with Gadamer and others) of the school leader.

We start this brief excursion into the question of power by qualifying it in the following way. We previously cited Bogotch's definition of leadership as "deliberate intervention that requires the moral use of power" (2000,   p. 2). Implicit in this definition is a concept of power that is not primarily or necessarily negative. Maxine Greene is also well aware of the positive connotations of power when she asks:

"What does it mean to be a citizen of the free world?" She concludes that it is "having the capacity to choose, the power to act to attain one's purposes, and the ability to help transform a world lived in common with others." (cited in Banks, 1991, p. 32)

Yet, in much social science writing, power is frequently equated with hegemony, with inequity, and with oppression. Hence, while we acknowledge that this may be the case, we agree with the implicit message of Bogotch's definition that this is not always true. Indeed, power, whether mechanical, personal, or communal, is the force that permits us to accomplish our goals, to act deliberately, and to achieve particular (and hopefully moral ends). Power (as Mintzberg [1983], pointed out) comes from the old French *poeir;* in its evolution, the French have used the same word, *pouvoir*, as the noun (power) and a verb (to be able). This sense of power as a force that enables, as in lights turning on or computers and automobiles running smoothly, is implicit in the orderly and satisfactory conduct of our daily lives.

When we use power in connection with people, we become (rightfully) more nervous. Perhaps our fearfulness is because we generally misquote Lord Acton's famous dictum, "Power tends to corrupt and absolute power corrupts absolutely" (Platt, 1993, p. 270), believing instead that all power corrupts. While we must take care to ensure that power does not oppress, repress, or marginalize others, we should also recognize its potential. The parent sitting in the principal's office in the Introduction would have been hard pressed to find that the principal had used his power wisely. But he could have. He could have listened, gained insight and understanding, and tried to make connections between the family and those who might have provided needed support and assistance. Carolyn began by using her power *over* Sonny inappropriately, but moved closer to a position of being *with*, one in which issues of power were subordinated to the developing relationship. While the educators in Hopeless High School may have been using their power inappropriately, blaming parents and students for the school's apparent lack of success, the educators in Mosaic Community School and those in Hopeful High School were trying to act deliberately and morally. Without realizing it, and certainly without meaning to, we misused our power when we introduced Michel to our graduate class one evening (as we will show in Chapter 5) in that we presented what we hoped would be a new voice, a perspective that would enhance the polyphony, but failed to do so in dialogic and relational ways.

Thus, with the qualification that educators use power on a daily basis and that it is incumbent on them to ensure that it is deployed morally, we return to an examination of ways in which power may, if used inappropriately in community situations, constrain dialogue. Here we suggest three aspects of power relations to which attention needs to be paid. The first is a reprise of the I-Thou discussion, the need for ensuring that because of power inequities, either real or imagined, we must relate to others as "Thou" and not "it." Second, we need to acknowledge our situatedness in roles, in contexts, and in cultures that perpetuate inequities in access to resources of many types. Third, we extend the concept of situatedness to focus on the need to understand how cultural and institutional norms and structures may constitute barriers to dialogue.

Subjugating "Subjects"

Near the end of his life, Foucault wrote:

> I would like to say, first of all, what has been the goal of my work during the last twenty years. It has not been to analyze the phenomenon of power, nor to elaborate the foundations of such an analysis. My objective, instead, has been to create a history of the different modes by which, in our culture, human beings are made subjects. (2000, p. 326)

Although Foucault does not use the word *situatedness*, he does introduce the relationships that we take up here—relationships between power and "subject." Foucault's use of the term *subject* is important for us to understand here, as it is in direct opposition to the ways in which we have already found it being used by Freire. Foucault uses "subject" (with a small s) much as Buber and others have used "it" to imply a dehumanized and objectified identity. Freire, on the other hand, advocates understanding a Subject (with a capital "S") as an agent of his or her own destiny, as a "Thou". He writes: "Dialogue is an I-Thou relationship, and thus necessarily a relationship between two Subjects" (2000a, p. 89). This contradictory employment of terminology can become confusing; hence, we shall attempt, in so far as possible, to avoid Foucault's use of "subject" while at the same time, as necessary, trying to capture his intent. Nevertheless, our focus is similar to that of Foucault: to investigate ways in which people exercise power inappropriately and hence treat others with less than absolute regard.

Here we do not intend to provide a catalogue of ways in which power is, or may be, misused in educational relations; that would not only be an endless endeavor, but one best undertaken by each of us individually and by each community collectively, taking into account its unique dynamics, cultures, and context. Here, we focus in broad strokes, on how power may be used positively to facilitate, or abused to inhibit and destroy, dialogic interactions.

We believe that understanding power relations hinges on making appropriate distinctions between I-it and I-Thou relations, between treating people as subjects (small s) and Subjects (capital S), or between treating people as objects or as human beings worthy of absolute regard. Moreover, being aware of the potential for the misuse or abuse of power is perhaps most important when interaction occurs between and among individuals from different formal positions in the hierarchy or from different social or cultural perspectives or among those with access to different types of information.

Freire (2000b) puts it this way:

> They are different experiences and as such they must be experienced differently. And because they are different, some can teach something to others, and some can learn something with the others. We learn only if we accept that others are different—otherwise, for example, dialogue is impossible. Dialogue can only take place when we accept that others are different and can teach us something we do not already know. (p. 212)

In other words, regardless of our differences, we can encounter each other in dialogic relationships *if* we accept that we have something to learn from other people, particularly because of the differences they may bring to the interaction.

Hence, despite the fact that, for the most part, the educators and parents from Mosiac Community School come from different social and cultural backgrounds and have different educational and occupational interests and experiences, they must make a choice. If the educators perceive the parents as generally less educated, less knowledgeable, and perhaps less supportive of the academic growth of their children, there will be no potential for a dialogic relation in that there will be a disposition to tell, to inform, or to advise, but little openness to learn from and with the parents. On the other hand, when the educators of Mosaic Community School approach the parents with a desire to understand them and to learn about their lived experiences, their hopes for themselves, and their aspirations for their children, then the ground is prepared for dialogue.

It is critical to note that here the goal really is understanding. It is not to find common ground (although that may happen), but to develop new insights, to bring our horizons closer together (to use Gadamer's metaphor), and to interact at the borders of our cultural experiences (as Bakhtin might argue). Freire (2000b), in talking of the differences between Europeans and Latin Americans, introduces yet another critically important idea—the notion of modesty:

> Europeans try to discover what there is in *common,* and that becomes essential for them, for me the essential is in the "differences," and, since each time I discover more differences, each time I become more aware of how little I know. That is the way of modesty, and it is the essential way. (p. 218)

Despite the fact that there may be differences in power in terms of formal positions as well as the knowledge and informal networks that various participants may access, the key to dialogue within a community is contained in Freire's word *modesty.* Another way of thinking about the disposition we must bring to dialogue within a community context is the notion of *humility.* If we remember constantly what, and how much, we do not know, it diffuses any sense of power *over* another and brings people into relationship simply to learn from each other. Modesty and humility, it seems to us, are at the heart of treating others with absolute regard, as Subjects, as Thou.

Moreover, when we recall the criteria introduced earlier, there can be neither community nor dialogue if we fail to deal justly, democratically, empathically, and optimistically with those with whom we live and work on a daily basis. Acknowledging the worth of others is fundamental to transformative education. We cannot educate objects, its, or subjects; we can only talk *about, at,* or *to* them, attempting to describe them, pour information into them, or manipulate them. Parker Palmer (1998) describes the futility of this approach beautifully: he says that we treat our students as "its," as patients, and that:

> The dominant diagnosis, to put it bluntly, is that our "patients" are brain-dead. Small wonder, then, that the dominant treatment is to drip data bits into our students' veins, wheeling their comatose forms from one information source to the next until the prescribed course of treatment is complete, hoping they will absorb enough intellectual nutrients to maintain their vital signs until they have graduated. (p. 41–42)

We can and must learn together as I, Thou, and Subject for the benefit of each of us individually as well as for the community as a whole.

Situating Selves

No matter how modest we attempt to be, as Gadamer clearly understood, individually we cannot divorce ourselves from our roles and collectively we cannot leave behind our culture and communities. Hence, we are always human beings, Subjects as Freire would call us, who are situated in various social, cultural, political, and economic structures and situations, with unique abilities, characteristics, and personal experiences that have shaped us. What is important for this investigation of the implications of the situatedness of power relations for dialogue is first and foremost that we become aware of our "prejudices" and acknowledge them. This is particularly important because of the implicit nature of most power inequities; they have more to do with patterns of behavior than with recognizable and identifiable utterances or acts.

Foster (1989) contends that

> educational leadership is always context bound. It always occurs within a social community and is perhaps less the result of "great" individuals than it is the result of human interactions and negotiations. Roosevelt and Churchill, to take two often-cited examples, took advantage of what might be called a "corridor of belief" which already existed in followers. Each leader did not so much create a new and idiosyncratic universe so much as enter these corridors and open various doors. (p. 44)

Foster is suggesting that the cultures within which leaders find themselves help to shape the relationships, interactions, and negotiations of leadership, not to mention achievements. There is no doubt this is true, as we have seen in Chapter One and elsewhere in this book. Leadership approaches and patterns—such as following the tenets of scientific management, of rule following, of blaming parents, or of focusing on the selection and adoption of new programs as the way to solve problems—do not develop and persist apart from the validation they receive in particular socio-cultural and political environments. Most commonly, leaders simply open existing doors and walk though them, unaware of the constraints, inequities, and challenges to be encountered on the other side.

Schneider (1995) says that:

> Diversity refers to the variety created in a society (and within any individual) by the presence of different points of view and ways of making meaning which generally flow from the influence of different cultural and religious heritages, from the differences in how we socialize men and women, and from the differences that emerge from class, age, and developed ability. (in Minnich, 1995, p. xx)

Yet, when we attempt to understand issues of power and how they may constrain dialogue, it is not enough to identify one's cultural, religious, or class origins. Many other invisible elements come into play. Here Foucault's work on surveillance and discipline is particularly useful. He recognizes that when one occupies a role that requires surveillance over others, one is expected to confirm that the others who are surveyed are behaving in accord with institutional expectations. The role itself permits one to stand in "normalizing judgment" over another and to know him or her in particular ways. Foucault (1995) describes the

> surveillance that makes it possible to qualify, to classify, and to punish. It establishes over individuals a visibility through which one differentiates them and judges them. In it are combined the ceremony of power and the form of the experiment, the deployment of force and the establishment of truth. (pp.184–185)

Hence, when educators are engaged in summative surveillance roles, when teachers invigilate an exam, when principals engage in formative supervision for the certification of a new teacher, or many other activities familiar to those who live and work in schools, they are not and cannot be involved in dialogic relationships. In these instances, their function is to maintain the norms of the institution, not to develop relationships and new understandings. Such a function, moreover, is a necessary part of every educator's role and is relatively common. Further, in the exercise of these legitimate functions related to one's job, it is not uncommon to acquire information about another that one might subsequently have occasion to use to maintain control over the other or to wield power in coercive ways to convince the other to act in certain ways that might be contrary to her principles or her self-interest.

Therein lies one of the difficulties of attempting to be both dialogic and accountable within institutional frameworks. As one gains information and knowledge about another person, one also gains power. And even the explicit acknowledgment of this power does not mitigate the application of this knowledge to serve the institution's ends.

How then can an educator whose very career brings her into unequal relationships with parents and students or an administrator whose position implies a supervisory role over other teachers ever be dialogical? Some would say that one cannot. Sidorkin (1999) states that "the power relations between teachers and students are inherently unequal" (p. 125). And in his subsequent book, he calls this inequality "tragic" (2002, p. 141). Moreover, he attributes a similar position to Buber, who, in discussing the therapeutic relation with Carl Rogers, says that equality is impossible because "You have necessarily another attitude to the situation than he has. You are able to do something he is not able. You are not equals and cannot be" (Sidorkin, 2002, p. 141).

In any given situation or relationship, it is most likely that one person will be able to do something the other will not or will have knowledge the other has not, and in this sense there will be an encounter of unequals. Yet, our concept of dialogue is not weakened by this challenge. Instead, we find in our notion of dialogue the best way to overcome this apparent difficulty.

The importance of acknowledging one's situatedness is, of course, a given. We acknowledged this necessity in Chapter Three in our discussion of understanding; here we assert that it holds equally true for relations in community. Any one who hopes to enter into a dialogic relation with another or with others must be acutely aware of those elements in his or her situation that might present a barrier to dialogue. The administrator, for example, is deeply embedded in the power relations of his or her institution, power that, to some extent, is constructed and maintained by its very invisibility. The power differential creates some very distinct differences between one who in some ways represents an institution and those who come seeking help or benefit from that institution (or alternatively those who may be punished by it).

It must be clearly stated again that not every interaction in these situations will be, or will need to be, dialogic. However, where the parties come together in modesty, out of a sure knowledge that there are things they do not know but that they may be able to learn from each other, a dialogic relation may exist. It is not the position, wealth, educational background, or social status of the parties that facilitates or constrains dialogue, but the commitment of all parties to bracket these elements and to meet the other as Thou, as fundamentally worthy of absolute regard.

At times, interactions may move between the dialogic and something more monologic in nature. An administrator cannot countenance a teacher's continued disregard for her students or the caustic comments, yelling, and swearing that one encounters on rare occasions in the school. Nor can he or she tolerate racist name-calling or bullying behaviors. Nevertheless, she may approach the requisite interaction with a dialogic attitude, one in which the self-esteem and Subjecthood of the other is kept securely in view. Here the administrator engages in a difficult, but important balancing act. She must encounter the other in an I-Thou relationship, seeking to understand and to develop new insights. But at the same time, the insights are teleological, not simply for the purpose of enhancing relationships (although that may occur), but also for the explicit purpose of changing behavior and even, on occasion, imposing necessary consequences. In such instances, the administrator is likely to move back and forth between the dialogic and the supervisory. Coexistent with the need for a satisfactory institutional resolution is the need for a personal encounter, one that leaves the other feeling he or she has been treated with absolute regard, while at the same time having been clearly told of the acceptable boundaries of the community.

The issue is not whether power relations and dialogue are able to coexist in organizational life, but how one discerns the appropriate time to depart from the immediately dialogical to assert monological, institution-oriented interactions. Though an avowed critic of the misuse of subjugating power in institutions like schools, Foucault noted, as have others to whom we have referred in this chapter, that power relations are inevitably a part of, and have their place in, a community. Foucault (2000) observed:

> A society without power relations can only be an abstraction. Which be it said in passing, makes all the more politically necessary the analysis of power relations in a given society, their historical formation, the course of their strength or fragility, the

conditions that are necessary to transform some or to abolish others. For to say that there cannot be a society without power relations is not to say either that those which are established are necessary, or that power in any event, constitutes an inescapable fatality at the heart of societies, such that it cannot be undermined. (p. 343)

The key is to determine which, if any, of our power relations is necessary or, at best, inevitable, to use them morally and deliberately for the good of others, and to hold in an extraordinary, unremitting tension with the dialogical all other uses of institutional power.

Situating ourselves, as educators, in our roles, experiences, and beliefs is one thing—attending to the power relations in the wider society is slightly different. Yet, when we attend to issues of justice, democracy, empathy, and optimism, we are addressing both. If our approach to educational leadership is grounded in bedrock principles related to the ethical use of power and to criteria for social justice and academic excellence, we will be guided by some benchmarks to ensure that our use of power is necessary, deliberate, and, above all, moral.

Social Structures

We saw earlier the extent to which we are shaped by our prejudices and situatedness, by the norms, values, beliefs, practices, and modes of thinking that have built up, sometimes over generations, to constitute what Bourdieu called our habitus (see Swartz, 1997, pp. 95–116). Habitus, as conceptualized by Bourdieu, "is inculcated in childhood and structured by the social context, becoming ingrained in the individual as both generative and transposable dispositions" (Swingewood, 1998, p. 95). Habitus both permits and preserves a sense of continuity with our past and constrains breaking free of past practices, even when they may be inequitable or unjust.

The problem is that we sometimes forget that the social world is largely of our own making and that we have the ability to re-form and re-create it. Thayer-Bacon puts this well. She says:

When we forget that social institutions are ones we have socially constructed and we can remake, we go beyond objectifying the world to reifying it as a fact, something that is fated. (2003, p. 83)

There is no doubt that social diversity is a reality; it exists within and grows from unequal ability on the part of both individuals and groups to access political, fiscal, social, cultural, and educational resources. As educators, we need not only to resist the notion that our institutions are immutable, but to take responsibility for instituting and implementing the needed liberating changes.

As we have seen, dialogue initiated from a genuine desire to understand the other is one starting point. We have also identified the need to situate ourselves. Yet, naming our position or situating ourselves does not lessen the power inequalities that continue to marginalize and minoritize others. For the dialogue to result in change, we must understand the ways in which power permits the inclusion and privileging of some people and the exclusion and marginalization of others. To some extent, this leads us to Bakhtin's concept of *polyphony* (the concept of multiple voices and perspectives, which we elaborate in Chapter Six). We need to be aware of which voices are being heard, who is at the table, and who is still silent and silenced—unable to participate in dialogue.

In other words, we cannot understand the inequities that exist within our communities without attending to difference, opening ourselves to it, and learning from it, through I-Thou relations with others. But we cannot understand more fully unless we ensure that more voices are also included. Deepening relations and understandings with a few is a wonderful and powerful starting point. Widening the circle of participants (as well as the range of ideas) is also essential.

Judith Green (1999) posits:

> Effective tolerance cannot be taught without teaching about the content of the differences to be tolerated. This content cannot be taught democratically without being taught sympathetically, and it cannot be taught sympathetically without acknowledgement and critical evaluation of the painful confrontations, power-structured lived relationships, and experiences of deeply damaging oppression that these differences have led to historically, continuing into our own times. (p. 65)

We would argue, following Bakhtin, that this deep understanding of others' experiences cannot be attained if we do not come into contact with those who have the knowledge and pain, those who have experienced power's oppression, for understanding happens at the borders of our lived experiences and cultural interactions. With Gadamer, we would argue that these understandings cannot occur without a fusing of our horizons, without deep relationships and increased understanding of new perspectives.

Through dialogue, we understand that power exists, not only in individuals, but in every educational organization, institution, and structure that is imbued with the power that is habitus. Lisa Delpit addresses this aspect of power in her seminal 1988 article, "The silenced dialogue: Power and pedagogy in educating other people's children."[2] Delpit maintains that every organization operates on the basis of (largely) unwritten rules that coincide with the rules of the dominant power group. She argues that there are five aspects to a "culture of power" that operate in ways that subjugate, exclude, and marginalize others (pp. 86–88). First, Delpit asserts, issues of power are enacted in classrooms. These include such issues as the power of the teacher over the students, the power of the curriculum to determine what counts as knowledge, and the power of legislators to determine "normalcy." Second, we need to recognize that the codes or rules for participating in power relate to how we (the dominant groups) talk, write, dress, and interact. Moreover, third, the rules of the culture of power are a reflection of the rules of those who already have power. In other words, middle- and upper-class English-speaking children are advantaged because the rules of the classroom are the rules they experience on a daily basis, while children from other cultures may learn a different set of rules at home and in their communities. Fourth, being told explicitly the rules of the culture of power makes both participation and acquiring power easier. Too often, well-intentioned educators try to overlook students' lack of understanding of the rules in an attempt to minimize discomfort, all the while hoping they will soon "get it." Yet, Delpit is clear that being told the rules is kinder, easier, and faster than being left to figure things out for yourself, as anyone who has struggled in a foreign culture has certainly experienced. Finally, she asserts that those with power are the least aware of and least willing to acknowledge its existence, while those without power are the most aware of its presence.

Acknowledging our power and "situatedness" is only the beginning. Helping others understand theirs, as well as ours, presents a considerable but important challenge for the educational leader wanting to build a deeply democratic, socially just, and inclusive community. By engaging in dialogic interactions, we believe the challenge can be profitably undertaken.

---

[2]   This framing of Delpit's argument is adapted from Shields (2003, pp.111–112).

Dialogue as the Foundation for Community

In this chapter, we have developed some criteria for assessing our progress toward developing the type of educational community that we might desire. We have not specified what community should be like or look like, because we believe there is no recipe, no one form that community can or should take. We have, however, suggested that there are several fundamental issues that need to be addressed, that might form the basis for numerous dialogic interactions in multiple sites, among numerous individuals, on an ongoing basis.

We have acknowledged that we live within multiple, layered, dynamic systems that both teach and provide for us and constrain and inhibit us. We have developed a framework of criteria for examining the educational systems within which we work and hope to make a difference for the children in our care—a framework that asks us to develop meanings that are just, democratic, empathic, and optimistic and that pay careful attention to the inevitable power structures and relationships within them to ensure they are as necessary and equitable as possible.

The systems within which we work are not value neutral. For that reason, it is imperative that the dialogue in which we engage acknowledges inequalities, brings them to our consciousness, and names and addresses them as we strive to forge new relationships of caring and understanding. Members of Mosaic Community School have stepped out courageously to implement changes. They will be more successful if they ground their attempts in dialogic understandings that include the criteria and considerations we have outlined here.

CHAPTER FIVE

Dialogue as Community Builder

The graduate course was well under way. We had been discussing the need for education to be socially just as well as academically excellent. The first few classes had included the familiar conversations, small group activities, demonstrations, role plays, and discussions of the readings. During the past few days, the instructors had spent time interacting with a visiting Israeli scholar– a blue-eyed Palestinian. We invited him to class, thinking it would provide an excellent opportunity for our North American students to hear about the "other side." So much of our press seemed to take the position that if only the Arab world would stop its violence and suicide bombings, then peace might be possible. There had been little reference in recent news media to the oppressive and discriminatory conditions under which many Palestinians lived in Israel.

We thought, too, that meeting Michel would be an excellent opportunity for the students to encounter alternative perspectives and to challenge their assumptions. After all, he did not look like the images of Palestinians with which we are presented in our press. He was not even Muslim, but Roman Catholic—another fact that we hoped would challenge our students' deeply rooted stereotypes.

Michel came and spoke to the class. He was calm, eloquent, and very persuasive. He spoke of the dual system of education in Israel, funded differently for Jewish and Palestinian students, of different curricula, and of different opportunities and restrictions in terms of career options and ability to move freely within the country. Our students were mesmerized; they asked numerous questions. We left that evening feeling that something significant had happened: our students had been presented with "difference"; they had met the "Other" in a way that was uncommon. They had heard a perspective that countered most of what they had been hearing and seeing in the national press.

But later, when Michel had returned to Israel and we were reading journals in which our students provided synthesis and comment on the course readings and activities, we came to understand that Richard, one of the most reflective and most thoughtful students in the class, had been deeply offended and acutely hurt. His father was a Holocaust survivor. Where was "his side" of the issue?

Where had we gone wrong? Should we not have created space for an alternative view? Should we not have given the students the opportunity to meet Michel? We had been trying to create a community that was open to difference even dissent, a community in which there was space for learning tolerance and respect for conflicting perspectives. And yet, one of our students had been dreadfully harmed. What should we have done differently?

***

We firmly believe that creating communities (whether in elementary or secondary schools or higher education) is central to developing contexts that are both socially just and academically excellent. We are convinced that educators must learn how to provide spaces in which people—all people— may bring their stories, their histories, their hurts, and their dreams; we must create communities in which all learn to listen—listen, as Delpit says, not only with their ears but with their hearts.

Yet, as we learned once again that evening, the task is difficult; conflicts, and disagreements, yes, and hurt may still occur. In this chapter, we focus on how dialogue is key to creating what we have called a deeply democratic *community of difference.* We show that, despite our awareness of the importance of dialogue, our belief in its power, and our attempts to create not only just, but dialogic classrooms, in the illustration above, we failed to employ dialogue in all of its power and potential. We will show how dialogue became crucial, not only to resolving the issues that Michel's presence provoked, but to deepening our understanding and to moving forward in the class.

In this chapter, we elaborate the need for, and concept of, school as a *community of difference* and then expand our concept of dialogue still further to demonstrate how it may enhance and facilitate, not only interpersonal interactions between two or three people, but larger social and organizational interactions as well.

Overcoming the "Dark Side" of Community

In recent years, many schools in developed countries have changed visibly. Their populations are now incredibly diverse—ethnically, socio-culturally, and socio-economically. There are more students from single-parent families, students who live with parents in same-sex relationships, and children who live with extended families, many members of which are first-generation immigrants. In North America, school policies and programs have been affected by these changes. There has been a remarkable increase of programs to increase awareness of racism, homophobia, and bullying. For a while, English as second language programs and bilingual programs proliferated, but most recently, social and political pressures and political backlash to bilingual education have reversed the trend in many districts.

Educational leaders have been challenged by the increasing diversity of their schools. Sometimes, we have met the challenges by building higher walls, protecting the norms, beliefs, and practices that have always existed, practices that have led some to talk about the dark side of community—the ways in which community not only unites but also excludes, marginalizes, and separates those who "belong" from those who do not.

Curriculum guides, textbooks, and testing agencies are increasingly influenced by what the major textbook companies have called "sensitivity and bias" guidelines, regulations that have, in fact, often worked to exclude anything controversial, any subject or substance that might cause offense, or even open communication about a myriad of issues. Ravitch (not particularly known for her social justice stance) has nevertheless become a sharp critic of guidelines that deny students the right to discuss topics like Mount Rushmore (it might offend the Lakota Indian group), the courage of a blind mountain climber (it implies that physically challenged people face more challenges), or Mary McLeod Bethune's 1904 school for girls (they were African American). Ravitch's book, *The Language Police* (2003), examines how the control of language has limited the scope of dialogue and defined what constitute appropriate topics for consideration, reading, discussion, and testing.[1] After an examination of the bias and sensitivity guidelines that control decisions about literature, language arts, and history texts and tests, she writes:

> The guidelines aim to create a new society, one that will be completely inoffensive to all parties; getting there, however, requires a heavy dose of censorship. No one asked the rest of us whether we want to live in a society in which everything objectionable to every contending party has been expunged from our reading materials. (p. 32)

Our response: we do not. She is right: no one asked us; no one initiated the dialogue. We have had no opportunity to assert that we want to live in a society in which we and our children are exposed to a myriad of cultures, beliefs, and practices, and we are sure that most of our fellow educators are in agreement about this. Eliminating all difference and dissent from our horizons ensures the perpetuation of the "dark side" of community. To counter these effects, many educators are working to create schools in which children are taught to reflect on perspectives other than their own, to understand them, and to respect those who hold disparate beliefs and engage in alternative practices. We advocate schools in which our children learn to evaluate, to weigh and to discriminate among various alternatives, and to apply criteria to help them assess the validity and worth of new perspectives.

The difficulty is for thoughtful educators to accept and advocate for the foregoing stance and to ensure the inclusion of difference without being accused of taking a relativistic stance that suggests "anything goes." It is therefore important to note that an accepting, respectful, inclusive stance does not imply that all beliefs, practices, customs, or perspectives are equally valuable and should be adopted without question into our school life or curriculum guides. It does require that each person be treated with "absolute

---

[1] It may be of interest to know that some of the topics that are objectionable include: owls; the school opened in Florida for African American girls in 1904 by Mary McLeod Bethune; legends about an "arrogant" king and a "selfish rich baker," a story about a "silly old lady," and a passage in which a rotting stump is metaphorically described as "an apartment house for the many different creatures of the forest" (p. 13).

regard" and that his or her position be heard and understood.

Eliminating all controversial issues would have made our task in the graduate class much easier: we would not have invited Michel to class. We would not have talked about the Arab-Israeli conflict or any ideas that might be sources of misunderstanding (such as racism or class structure). But that would simply have played into the need for consensus, for agreement, and for complicit silence about important and difficult issues that contain within them the potential for conflict that may even cause pain and offense. If we do not come to grips with conflict and difference in our school communities, where will children learn to live in a richly diverse world?

Deeply Democratic Communities of Difference

In the past two decades, much has been made of the need for schools to become communities. In 1993, Sergiovanni actually issued a call for a change of metaphor, saying that if we stopped thinking about schools as organizations and began thinking about them as communities, we could actually change the lived reality for students. As Shields (2003) stated, "theoretical attention has been paid to notions of professional communities (Louis, 1996), learning communities (Dufour, 2001; Mitchell, 1999), online communities (Powers & Barnes, 2001), value communities (Vendler, 2001), communities of hope (Neugebauer, 2000), and communities of memory (Bellah et al., 1985), to name but a few" (p. 34).

With all the attention given to *community* in the educational literature, the term began to be used everywhere (much like the word *dialogue*) and consequently, began to lose much of its initial appeal. Some scholars became disenchanted with the use of the word. Some rejected the ideal of community altogether, believing it is simply a quest for unity and sameness. Outside of the educational community, Iris Marion Young (1990) saw in it an entity that "denies and represses social difference," one that desires instead "the fusion of subjects with one another which in practice operates to exclude those with whom the group does not identify" (p. 227). Young then advocated rejecting the ideal of community and replacing it with the metaphor of the "city." She wrote, "I propose to construct a normative ideal of city life as an alternative to both the ideal of community and the liberal individualism it criticizes as asocial" (p. 237). City life, as Young described it, is composed of clusters of people who do not know each other, but who venture beyond familiar enclaves to meet and interact (p. 237). Young claims that her vision of a city evokes images of people who are from diverse backgrounds, with very different perspectives on the world, living harmoniously in close proximity to one another. Yet, we are uncomfortable with this description of a community; living in close proximity neither implies nor necessitates the relationships and understandings we think are foundational to community.

Despite our discomfort with Young's proposal, we do not disagree that some images of community focus exclusively on what is shared and on how to help those who differ to fall into line, learning the required norms and sharing the requisite values. These homogeneous concepts of community, however, are not what we envisage when we talk about a deeply democratic school community. For that reason, we speak of a *community of difference*. We are not conceptualizing an entity that is created by overlooking, minimizing, or marginalizing different perspectives. Indeed, in a publicly mandated entity such as schools, that would likely be an impossible task, even if it were desirable, which we believe it is not.

The strength of public schooling—its beauty, complexity, and challenge—is its diversity. When we create public institutions in countries that are organized around democratic principles, we are acknowledging that the institutions will serve people with a rich variety of views, cultures, needs, and potential contributions. When we mandate attendance of minor children at these institutions (for a minimum of 10 years), we are making a commitment to find ways to acknowledge, respect, and incorporate their diversity into the very fabric of the public institution. To do otherwise would be to suggest that some citizens have greater rights to self-determination, to expression, and to participation than others—concepts we categorically reject in Western democracies.

Hence, our concept of a school community is one in which individuals come together as whole people, bringing their diverse perspectives, practices, cultures, beliefs, values, and traditions into the "space" that will become a community. It is then the responsibility of those within the community, and particularly of the educational leaders, to facilitate the conditions under which a community may develop. This type of leadership, we believe, must be firmly grounded in an understanding of dialogue consistent with Burbules' (1993) description:

> Dialogue is not fundamentally a specific communicative form of question and response, but at heart a kind of *social relation* that engages its participants. A successful dialogue involves a willing partnership and cooperation in the face of likely disagreements, confusions, failures, and misunderstandings. Persisting in this

process requires a relation of mutual respect, trust, and concern—and part of the dialogical interchange often must relate to the establishment and maintenance of these bonds. The substance of this interpersonal relation is deeper, and more consistent, than any particular communicative form it may take. (p. 20, emphasis in original)

Dialogue, Burbules says, is a *social relation* that engages us. As we have seen previously, according to Burbules, successful dialogue fulfills three "rules" or guiding principles: participation, commitment, and reciprocity. It requires our participation in the lives of those with whom we come into contact, those with whom we work on a daily basis. It demands commitment to persist in the face of misunderstanding, hurt, and failure. It requires reciprocity or mutuality, a listening back-and-forth response. It requires hard work and trust. Our experience with Richard's hurt after Michel's presentation led us into dialogue, a dialogue that we ultimately shared with, and opened to, the whole class.

The Problems of Community

One of the great difficulties with creating schools that are deeply democratic communities is that education, as a formal institution, has such a long history. As we have seen, the French sociologist Bourdieu developed the concept of *habitus* to explain why and how ideas and practices persist for a long time. He posited, as part of his explanation for social reproduction, that habitus is a sort of socialized subjectivity, "not a habit but a system of 'durable dispositions' or properties which allow agents to understand, interpret and act in the social world" (Swingewood, 1998, p. 950). In Bourdieu's words, habitus is a

system of durable, transposable dispositions, structured structures predisposed to function as structuring structures, that is, as principles which generate and organize practices and representations that can be objectively adapted to their outcomes without presupposing a conscious aiming at ends or an express mastery of the operations necessary in order to attain them. (Swartz, 1997, p. 100–101)

Our systems of education, i.e., our schools, and the ways in which they are organized, structure our thinking. Moreover, if our internal structures advantage and include some people and disadvantage or exclude others, they may do so, not as a result of conscious discrimination, but Bourdieu suggests, because of the durable dispositions that have been developed by our schooling processes and sustained over time.

Bourdieu also introduced the concept of *field* as a "network, or configuration, of objective relations between positions" as "structured spaces that are organized around specific types of capital or combinations of capital" (Swartz, 1997, p. 117). Hence, fields such as law, education, religion, and politics all "consist of clusters of patterned activities centered around basic social functions" (Swartz, p. 120). Although in Bourdieu's conception, fields are not fixed but are sites of struggle and resistance; "within the logic of reproduction, they seldom become sites of social transformation" (Bourdieu & Passeron, 1977, p. 121).

Bourdieu's concepts of fields and habitus help us to understand how tradition tends to continue to shape beliefs and actions so that existing opportunity structures are perpetuated and social and cultural practices continue to be reproduced over time rather than changed. Beliefs and practices are internalized, transmitted intergenerationally, and hence, tend to circumscribe what we (as a society) have come to believe is natural, reasonable, or possible in any given field. Communities, in a homogeneous and traditional sense, only perpetuate the problems of social stratification and exclusion because that is the way their members have come to think about themselves in relation to others.

Gramsci used the term *hegemony* to describe the way in which dominant values may combine to maintain certain practices. Swingewood (1998) explains how this concept of hegemony suggests

> a field of forces in which the various components resist harmonious integration into a social whole, so that partly autonomous forces at work…constitute the context of collective class action and the formation of consciousness. (p. 21)

Swingewood qualifies this statement by saying that while this enables Gramsci to theorize alternative and competing forces, it is at its root, constrained by history and tradition:

> Gramsci's formulations suggest a closed element in which the autonomy of practices and the autonomy of culture are circumscribed by the logic of history, which points inevitably to the succession of bourgeois hegemony by proletarian hegemony. (1998, p. 21)

The challenge for educators, therefore, is to find ways to break out of the hegemony, out of the constraints of habitus that actually function below the level of consciousness, in order to effect social change.

Breaking Free...

We are suggesting that a new understanding of democratic community with a deep sense of the importance of relationships within that community and of the role dialogue plays in advancing both understanding and relationship is a way forward. In fact, we believe that it is the concept of dialogue that permits us to move beyond the habitus and hegemony of history and to discover a sense of agency that permits us to effect change.

The community that we advocate is not the community circumscribed by history and traditions, although it is critically important not to lose sight of the historical roots of our institutions. Nor is it a community which excludes those who bring other histories, other interpretations of history. Rather, our concept of community is built on, and out of, diversity. Further, acknowledging the diversity of our institutions is quite different from ensuring that the diversity is recognized and incorporated in meaningful ways. In the forward to Minnich's (1995) discussion of diversity in higher education, Carol Schneider writes:

> From the beginning then, the United States cast its lot both with heterogeneity as a defining characteristic and with dialogue and deliberation as democratic resources for the resolution of difference. Yet from the beginning as well, this historic commitment to a republic of reasoning was constrained and contradicted by the expectation that in this society founded on participatory citizenship, the citizens participating should be white and male. (p. x)

Unfortunately, it is not only in the United States where we find that the *rhetoric* of democracy and dialogue has surpassed the meaningful *practice* of full inclusion and participation. We acknowledge that there has been attention paid in most democratic societies to issues of diversity and lip service paid to the need for dialogue and understanding. Nevertheless, we are also convinced of the need to reconceptualize democratic community in ways that move diversity and dialogue to the center.

Judith Green (1999) speaks of a "mistaken premise that the ideal of community is inextricably tied into [a] hopeless quest for unity and totality" (p. 2). She advocates instead what she calls "deep democracy," democracy that involves

> respecting, communicating receptively, and cooperating with those whose values are different than but not unalterably antagonistic to one's own. (p. 60)

The notion of different but not unalterably antagonistic brings us to the issue of relativism. There are bounds to community; there are bounds to what behaviors and practices are to be tolerated. In a school community, while we communicate to students the need for *absolute regard* for persons, we cannot permit *behavior* that endangers any child. While we urge discussion of both Israeli and Palestinian historical claims to their holy cities and to ownership of land, we cannot condone the *practice* of suicide bombing that destroys innocent victims. But such decisions must be made within the context of a given community and through the understanding and practice of dialogue as we have developed it in the first section of this book. As Kierstead (1993) noted, "the problem with all forms of ethical relativism is that they diminish the importance of moral discourse" (p. 4). Bakhtin, in fact, argues the same point. If there is no need to treat people with absolute regard, if there is no need to come to an understanding of their position, there is no need to talk about differences at all. Yet, this will not lead to the type of deeply democratic *community of difference* we believe should exist in schools.

Dialogue as a Cornerstone of Community

Community is made up of people who come together, bringing diverse, sometimes oppositional histories and perspectives. It is developed from a myriad of small interpersonal interactions, built up over time, resulting in new relationships of respect and understanding and in the development of shared understandings about appropriate collective action. In order to make meaning from the diverse perspectives that constitute a community, dialogue has often been posited as a desirable approach.

Some, as we have seen in this book, write about the importance of dialogue in the creation of a new type of more equitable, inclusive, and respectful community. Minnich cites Benjamin Barber who states that "in the absence of community, there is no learning...language itself is social, the product as well as the premise of sociability and conversation" (1995, p. xxi). She then writes:

> Dialogue becomes absolutely critical to this generative, relational democracy, and the civic nature becomes not simply a political process, or a marketplace of competing interests, but rather one that seeks deliberately to reflect and address the aspirations, needs, and realities of all of its citizens. (p. 33)

Over and over, we find writers who advocate dialogue, relationship, and understanding, but who use the terms without elaboration, seeming to suggest that the definitions are clear, almost implying that change will be realized as we invoke the concepts. We know, however, that this is not the case. We know that despite the relationships we had already built with our students, despite our attempts to advance understanding through the presentation of Michel's alternative perspective, despite the opportunity we created for "dialogue"—for questions, answers, and discussion—something went wrong.

To better understand what dialogue is and what it can do in a social context, we return to Bakhtin's notion of dialogue. We cited his belief in the ontology of dialogue in Chapter Two: for Bakhtin, to live means to participate in dialogue, to invest oneself in discourse that enters into the fabric of one's existence. It is to live in openness to difference, encountering difference and listening to its multiple voices.

Characteristics of Dialogue

Bakhtin introduces three additional concepts we now take up: *outsideness, heteroglossia,* and *polyphony*. Each of these offers guidance and insight to the educational leader wanting to understand how to build a socially just community.

Outsidedness

We introduced the concept of *outsidedness* in Chapter Two to indicate a need for some degree of distance, for enough separation between the one who is trying to understand and the one who is being understood such that each stands within his or her own identity. Bakhtin (1986b) talks about the need for an "*open* unity" (p. 6) and states that "it is immensely important for the person who understands to be *located outside* the object of his or her creative understanding—in time, in space, in culture" (p. 7). This is because

> in the realm of culture, outsidedness is a most important factor in understanding. It is only in the eyes of *another* culture that foreign culture reveals itself fully and profoundly.... A meaning only reveals its depths once it has encountered and come into contact with another, foreign meaning: they engage in a kind of dialogue, which surmounts the closedness and one-sidedness of these particular meanings, these cultures. (p. 7)

Dialogue permits us to understand meanings and cultures that are not our own. They do not become ours. We do not become the other, but by meeting at the boundaries rather than where ideas have become enclosed, the potential exists for understanding. In this way, dialogue moves us beyond the fields and habitus identified by Bourdieu, beyond the hegemony of Gramsci, to the borders where new understandings may develop.

Heteroglossia and Polyphony

Heteroglossia is the term Bakhtin introduced to describe the multiplicity of everyday languages—not simply language groups as in French, English, and Punjabi, but languages as in the speech (words and content together) of the rich, the poor, the outcast, the privileged, and so forth. His belief was that while we, as individuals, are bound into social groups, even within those groups (e.g., a nation), one finds a multiplicity of perspectives that exist as different communities listening and speaking to one another. Heteroglossia acknowledges the existence of multiple, autonomous positions that coexist through a process of dialogic interaction. Through heteroglossia, both language and diverse meanings remain alive, developing and dynamic. Meaning is never fully contained within one voice, within one individual, but is created through dialogue and interaction among multiple voices.

Polyphony is the presence of the viewpoint (position) of the others, whether the voices are actually present or not. If we are to have anything other than a monologic utterance, we require polyphony. If we are having a conversation about a controversial topic (perhaps the Middle East situation) and we recognize that a particular perspective is missing, it is important to actually attempt to voice it. Polyphony helps us to understand the difference between the positivist notion of Truth (with a capital T) and truths. For Bakhtin, no one person holds Truth. Truth cannot be contained within a single consciousness. Sidorkin (1999) elaborates:

> Bakhtin does not mean to say that many voices carry partial truth.... A statement like "the truth is somewhere in the middle," is not at all what Bakhtin had in mind. He apparently had a very different conception of truth. Truth reveals when one can hear and comprehend both or all voices simultaneously, and more than that. When one's own voice joins in and creates something similar to a musical chord. (p. 30)

In this conception, there is no single truth (that belongs to the deity), but rather, there are multiple truths, truths that can never be fully grasped.

Indeed, no single voice is capable of telling (or representing) truth. Truth requires listening to a multiplicity of voices (polyphony). Sidorkin (2002) illustrates: if I hear two people discuss their relationship, I can grasp some truth about their relationship, although this truth is not to be summarized into a monological description" (p. 98). The truth about the relationships is not "owned" by either party, but is most fully expressed in dialogue between the two.

Bakhtin (1973) relates the capacity to produce truth to the multiplicity of voices that deliver the message, or rather a number of messages. At the end of this book, he writes:

> To be means to communicate dialogically. When dialogue is finished, all is finished .... Everything else is the means, the dialogue is the end. One voice alone concludes nothing and decides nothing. Two voices is the minimum for life, the minimum for existence. (p. 213)

Once again, as illustrated in Figure 1, we find here the conviction of the fundamental ontology of relationships and dialogue. Without them, there is no life, as Bakhtin sees it.

Sidorkin (2002) identifies three principles related to Bakhtin's polyphony: perpetuity, mutual addressivity, and inclusion (p. 159). Dialogue itself is polyphonic and never ending. In it, "the voices never merge, never achieve a formal consensus, and if such consensus arises, it is a by-product" (p. 159). Dialogue requires multiple voices that present themselves to each other and define themselves in relation to each other, and not in relation to predetermined concepts they wish to communicate. Dialogue requires a concerted attempt to ensure that all relevant voices are included.

Green (1999) suggests, in a somewhat more instrumental vein, that "the social inquiry process must include as equals those affected by its results if it is to build the mutual trust that makes it possible both to elicit the widely dispersed, necessary information only diverse participants can contribute" (p. 44). Here, the goal of the inclusion as she sees it is to build mutual trust to solicit information necessary to reach some social resolution, even if temporary and fragile. In talking about the commonalities of human existence as well as the differences that exist across cultures, Green elaborates:

> If such commonalities are to matter, they cannot be stipulated, but must be discovered or negotiated through a cooperative, cross-difference process of information-seeking and understanding-building that results in a cultivated

pluralism that will change some customary self-understandings and destabilize some existing, power-structured relationships with others in the process. (p. 122)

Bakhtin and Sidorkin would likely disagree with the teleological (purposeful) focus, but not with the outcome. For Bakhtin, dialogue is simply fundamental to life itself. The voices never merge, never come to a consensus that in any way resembles a grand narrative, meta-theory, or the Truth. Yet, as Sidorkin (2002) asserts, this "does not in any way mean that the voices do not change each other. Quite to the contrary, the interaction is the truest moment of their being. To be changed is the destiny of all meanings we produce" (p. 170). The issue is simply that we must avoid the dangers of believing we have been fully understood or that we have understood fully and that there is therefore no need for further understanding, for such a conviction would shut down dialogue.

Rutherford (1990) argues this point as well, stating that when one believes that one has attained Truth and that one's particular truth is universal, then we have become undemocratic:

> So the recognition of a plurality of truths is only a starting point. It in turn must be governed by what David Held has called the principle of democratic autonomy.... Democratic autonomy implies a respect and tolerance for other people's needs as the guarantee of your own freedom to choose. Groups and communities become potentially undemocratic, as fundamentalists of whatever flavour do, when they begin to proclaim the universal truth of their particular experience. (p. 98)

My experience is my starting point, one lens through which I begin to make sense of the world. Yours is another. Together we can create new understandings out of which we may be changed. But, a further caution: if we consider that the new understanding is somehow final, the ultimate truth, we are not only shutting down future dialogue, we are suggesting that those voices that we have not heard have nothing useful or valid to add. They have become *it,* rather than *Thou*, objects rather than Subjects.

To go back to the graduate class, final, ultimate Truth does not reside in Michel's words or position, nor in Richard's, nor in our comments as instructors. There are many truths to be discovered when we provide an opportunity for differences to come together and to interact. One lesson we had to learn that night was about the multiplicity of truths. The past trauma of Richard's father as a Holocaust survivor and Richard's relationship with him constituted one deeply significant and valid truth. The present reality of Michel's experience of discrimination and marginalization was another. Our desire to increase understanding constituted a third truth. Each person in the class developed a different understanding from the interaction of these three "voices," understandings that themselves became changed as they were expressed in the ongoing dialogues of the classroom and beyond. Yet Richard was still puzzled, upset, stressed, and distressed.

Does that mean we should not have introduced Michel and his lived experience to our class? Were we simply using our power as instructors to impose a position on our students and to introduce dissonance into the conversation?

Dialogue and Dissonance

Bakhtin (1973), in his introduction to the second edition of his exploration of Dostoevsky's poetics, wrote:

> It is hardly necessary to mention that the polyphonic approach has nothing in common with relativism (nor with dogmatism). But it should be noted that both relativism and dogmatism equally exclude all argumentation and all genuine dialogue, either by making them unnecessary (relativism) or impossible (dogmatism). (p. 56)

The difficult task for educators is to engage in authentic dialogue, dialogue that avoids relativism, as well as dialogue (or at least interaction, for it would not be true dialogue) that results in dogmatic understandings. Had we chosen not to introduce Michel to our class, we might have been accused of dogmatism, accepting by our assent the predominant western view of the situation in Israel. Introducing him as just another voice might have led to a dangerous and reductive relativism. Yet, despite our, and Michel's, best attempts at presenting Michel's perspectives as an invitation to dialogue, as one truth to be engaged with others in a polyphonic quest for truth, he came to the class in a position of power—a noted visiting scholar—and students (not incorrectly) interpreted his position as legitimate, perhaps even the one the instructors considered most legitimate. Thus, the issue of power returns to the table as we wrestle with how educators can facilitate and model dialogue and live dialogically.

Madeleine Grumet (1995), in writing about curriculum, advances a definition that goes well beyond the texts we normally think of. She begins by emphasizing that our "relationships to the world are rooted in our relationships to the people who care for us" (p. 19). She focuses her attention on the implications of this realization for the educational process itself. This leads her to make the case that "curriculum is never the text, or the topic, never the method or the syllabus"; but curriculum is "the conversation that makes sense of ... things.... It is the process of making sense with a group of people of the systems that shape and organize the world we can think about together" (p. 19).

As educators, we have likely come to accept the oft-stated position that curriculum is complex and multiple, that it consists of the formal (that which is written in approved guides), the informal (that which is assumed through it), and the hidden (that which, like habitus, is so entrenched that it operates at an unconscious level to include some topics, ideas, and voices and to marginalize others (see, for example, English, 2003; Shields, 2003). But we often fail to acknowledge the power relations that tend to privilege some forms of information and devalue others, that make conversations to make sense of things some of the most difficult tasks of educators and educational leaders today.

We have seen, as we wrestled with dialogue as a form of understanding, that people in institutions are vested with varying degrees of formal and informal power. A mother who enters the principal's office (as we saw in our earlier example) does not come believing that the principal can divest himself or herself of institutional authority or responsibility to administer rules in a fair and judicious way. But she can hope, and expect, that she will be treated with "absolute regard," that her position will be heard, and that an attempt will be made to understand rather than to judge. Sonny did not come to my home that day after school believing that we had suddenly become friends or that, when I left the school, I also divested myself of my "teacher" identity.

Buber (1988) recognized the reality of context when he wrote, "You are not equals and cannot be...of course there are limits to simple humanity.... I see you *mean* being on the same plane, but you cannot" (p. 162). And there is no doubt, we cannot be equals in every respect. Yet, somehow, if we understand dialogue as Bakhtin advocates it, the inequality of positions is overshadowed by polyphony, "the principle of engaged co-existence of multiple yet unmerged voices" (Sidorkin, 2002, p. 145). The need to hear and understand another takes precedence over considerations of power or position and social or cultural capital. In essence, it provides a way forward, a way to ensure that multiple voices and perspectives are heard in a school community.

As we saw in Chapter Two, dialogue does not necessitate liking; nor is it a synonym for empathy. We enter into dialogue because it is a moral and ontological imperative, not because we have entered into an emotional relationship with another person. The need to engage in dialogue is powerful. In examining Plato's allegory of the cave, Liston (2001) observes that the "path to enlightenment is not necessarily happy or painless; in fact it can be quite confusing" (p. 189). This is important. Dialogue is not always, certainly not necessarily, enjoyable, easy, or comforting; it can be difficult; it can evoke pain and discomfort. While we might want to contest Plato's view of a single path, asserting that there may be multiple paths to enlightenment, we do not assume that any of the paths that lead to deeper relationship and increased understanding are free from the potential for conflict and confusion. Liston elaborated:

> In schools, this would mean that each student, teacher, or administrator would recognize that "in order for me to be me, I must engage in relationship with others, who must maintain separate identities as they relate to me."... I am only me within the context of our relationship which makes me, me and you, you. (p. 209)

Sharing our contexts and identities and developing relationships involves risk—risk of being misunderstood or hurt; but it also embraces hope—hope for stronger and deeper school communities.

Concluding Comments

The discerning reader must have been screaming that when we introduced Michel to our class, despite good intentions, despite a desire to introduce polyphony and to acknowledge heteroglossia, we were not acting dialogically. We did introduce him out of a desire to provide a different, poignant, and knowledgeable voice that, we believed, might counter some of the myths and misinformation often reported in our press. We introduced him in the hope that our students would be able to understand that they might not have heard all relevant voices, that they might come to know how partial their understanding was.

But we ignored the other half of the equation. We did not introduce Michel into our class in the context of relationships. His became a monologic lecture, followed by a too brief time of questions and answers that might have become dialogic had we created adequate space and allocated sufficient time for relationship. There was no to-and-fro play, no capacity for reciprocal encounter, no opportunity for Richard and Michel to engage each others' situatedness. Talk, even in the context of presenting important and missing information, is not dialogue.

As the course proceeded, the instructors spent many hours discussing our failings. We acknowledged that we had not done anything wrong. We granted that having our students meet Michel was important. We agreed that the information had been essential—even at the risk of opening wounds and making those for whom the dominant position was comfortable feel uneasy. But we also accepted responsibility for what we had not done. We had not offered students any opportunity to know what was coming or to reflect on their positions; we had not provided any points of connection to previous classes, beyond the explanation that in a *community of difference*, it is important to hear various and diverse positions and to treat each person with absolute regard. We believed that we were contributing to the "conversation that makes sense of things." Yet we had not created adequate space to explore both the well-known, dominant perspective and the lesser known, minority perspective. We had presented information (yes, in the physical body of a person) in a monologic, not a dialogic way. And, during the last session of the course, as we offered the students in the class an opportunity to comment on what they had learned, we shared what we had learned as well.

Dialogue as the Basis for Community

We have learned an important lesson. We have come to understand, through our analysis of a good intention gone wrong, that dialogue is the basis for relational ontology and epistemology and that being and understanding are fundamental to the creation of a *community of difference*— a sense of school community forged out of the norms, beliefs, values, perspectives, and practices of all of its members. One half of the coin is not enough. Understanding and relationship go hand in hand. Minnich (1995) recognized it when she wrote:

> Our vision is one of *relational* pluralism, wherein we acknowledge, affirm, and find strength in our singularities while at the same time maintaining connections with others in intersecting circles of community, large and small. (our emphasis, p. xxi)

Relational pluralism relies first on relationships and then on understanding our singularities and differences, but never at the expense of severing our connections from other, intersecting circles of which we are a part.

> Bakhtin sees language as "the means whereby different social groups represent ideological values and affirm their cultural, political and social aspirations *in relation to others*." (our emphasis, Swingewood, 1998, p. 123)

Again, we see the emphasis on relationships. Language is not just words, but words in relationship. There is no meaning elsewhere, as we have seen. We asked Michel to present a position, but forgot that it needed to be done in relation to others.

Thus, we return to the concept of absolute regard for the other, a regard that requires both relationship and understanding as the basis for developing new social norms, for breaking out of the habitus of schooling, and for finding new ways to make sense of things, whether topics in the formal curriculum or outside it. For herein lies the essence of a community that is able to embrace all of its members and to ensure that all members can listen and be heard, that they have the opportunity to construct new understandings and to contribute to the understanding of others.

Our school communities are richly diverse, but when we fail to encounter the diversity in openness and understanding, our fixed and monologic snapshots limit us and prevent us from encountering the colorful, swirling kaleidoscope of diverse meanings. A deeply democratic community in which people may live, work, learn, and grow together depends on multiple dialogic moments.

Bakhtin described the "self as the 'gift of the other' constituted in and through discourse as productive practice" (Swingewood, 1998, p. 124). We can think of no greater gift for the educational leader to bestow on his or her school than this vision of community, grounded in deep democracy and dialogic action.

CHAPTER SIX

Carnival—A Catalyst for Re-Creating Community and Rejuvenating Dialogue

The time was 1:30 p.m. It was the last afternoon before the Christmas holiday period at Urban High School. The high school was alive with people, greeting each other, wishing each other "Happy Holidays," and chattering in anticipation of the big event. The gymnasium was buzzing with excitement. The stands were overflowing with exuberant students, voices raised in a cacophony of sound. More were milling around on the floor, trying to find seats, and calling and gesticulating to get their friends' attention. Decorations adorned the walls; the school band played with enthusiasm; students stood, clapping, whistling, and cheering as the performers entered.

First up were members of the Students Council. Some took the roles of teachers, parodying their behaviors; others played the parts of some of the most famous and infamous student—star athletes, members of the band, heroes of the smoking area—all came up for reward or punishment at the hands of the would-be teachers. Hilarity rang through the gymnasium as the students mimicked the best-known phrases, gestures, dress, and hair-dos of those teachers singled out in this year's presentation. As the skit came to an end, students cheered, stomped, clapped, and shouted for more.

Then it was the teachers' turn. One group, the readers, took its place in front of a line of microphones. Others manned the sound and light systems. Still others, extravagantly costumed (some in drag), stood nervously in the wings, awaiting their entrance cues with anticipation. The melodrama began; the intricate twists of plot drew the audience in, with boos, hisses, jeers, and cheers growing more frantic as the suspense heightened. Mr. Swartz, as usual, was the villain, Mr. Bianco, the dashing hero, and Miss Dolce, the beautiful, bashful heroine. Sally, the popular student council president (played by Mrs. Elder), was involved with Mr. Swartz, cleverly scheming to discredit Miss Dolce to gain Mr. Bianco's attentions for herself. Conrad, the senior basketball captain (played by Mr. Connolly) grabbed his smelly Nikes to help to overpower Swartz as the first act concluded.

***

This vision of a high school gym overcrowded with excited students is more typical of a basketball tournament than a semester-closing assembly. Why had the students not skipped out, especially when attendance at the Christmas assembly was neither mandatory nor monitored? Why did the students spend hours preparing a skit that had the potential to expose, embarrass, or annoy some of their teachers? And what of the teachers? Why had Mr. Nimmins and Mr. Yale spent countless hours writing a script and taping music? And how did they ever convince the principal to dedicate the December staff meeting to a rehearsal of the teachers' play?

And yet, the annual celebration was an eagerly awaited occurrence at Urban High School—anticipated as much by the teachers for the role they might be asked to play, gently and publicly teasing some of the most infamous students, as by the students for the opportunity to both tease the teachers and see them dressed in outlandish costumes in the annual Christmas melodrama. Can we quickly set aside such an event as a foolish waste of time and energy, a missed opportunity for meaningful instruction and on-task academic learning? Or does such a quick dismissal of the annual assembly miss some deeper significance it might hold in the life of the school?

Despite times of satisfaction and visible progress, there are moments when, as educational leaders, we feel we have reached an impasse. No matter what we try, people are sometimes still at odds with one another; there is frustration with outside pressures, new policies, and increased measures of accountability. Nothing seems to be working. In this chapter, we examine ways in which introducing playfulness and carnival into dialogue may help us to break free of our stifling educational habitus, overcome the fetters that frustrate us, and move forward more positively. Here, we argue that dialogue is not only generative of relationships and understanding (as we have demonstrated in the previous chapters), but creative and re-creative. We come to a realization of the ability of dialogue to create, change the cultures, recreate the structures, and alter the power relations in schools—all elements that sometimes stand as barriers to meaningful community and to a more equitable social order.

In this chapter, we present a rationale for, and image of, dialogue as playful, inventive, and carnivalesque. We hasten to add the qualifier that carnival is not necessarily the permanent state that we envisage in any educational organization; moreover, dialogue can certainly exist without carnival, but at the same time, we believe that no dialogic leader should ignore the significant potential of playfulness and carnival.

The Seriousness of Play

As we saw in our earlier examination of dialogue as understanding, Gadamer used play as a means for describing the process of dialogue. Play and playfulness have also long been subjects of interest for child psychologists. Christie (1980), in a review of the cognitive significance of children's play, defined play as behavior that "(1) has no extrinsic goals, (2) is spontaneous and voluntary, (3) is pleasurable, and (4) involves active engagement on the part of the participant" (p. 24). The parallels between Christie's definition of play and our concept of dialogue become immediately apparent. Dialogue, too, is engaged in not for a specific purpose, but for its intrinsic worth. It is spontaneous, requiring commitment and openness, but cannot be coerced. The pleasure derived from deep interpersonal relationships, from understanding and being understood, endures far beyond the moment of the exchange in which the connection with another takes place. And of course, there can be no dialogue without participation and engagement, willingness to meet another in an inherently meaningful encounter.

Christie described with some concern what he saw as an increasing rejection of play in early childhood programs and a concomitant emphasis on "direct instruction in academic skills" (p. 23). Yet, the evidence he reviewed from correlational, experimental, and play-training studies demonstrated the importance of play in enhancing children's divergent thinking abilities, problem-solving capabilities, and verbal intelligence. He cites an early study by Dansky and Silverman (1977) who found:

> Playful activity can provide children with an opportunity to organize their experiences and exercise their cognitive abilities in a manner that is likely to facilitate imaginative adaptations to future situations. (p. 26)

Play and playfulness provide the basis for young children to be more able to adapt to new situations in the future. Play then also constitutes one of the fundamental ways of teaching the openness that we have shown is central to dialogic leadership and interaction.

The importance of play is so well recognized that psychologists often use a technique known as play therapy to help children express their feelings, gain a sense of power over their circumstances, and develop social skills. Play therapy permits children to determine the rules and to change the direction of the play as they desire. It permits them to master frightening feelings and allows children to create an imaginary world in which they feel a sense of control (Walmsley & Associates, 2003).

In organizations, too, many people feel helpless and fearful, oppressed by the structures and cultures of power with which they are confronted on a daily basis. We believe that organizational "play," even though it may not be instituted or supervised by trained therapists, can help to breakdown institutional barriers and permit people to participate more fully in the dialogue of organizational life.

In 1976, James March developed an argument for what he called "the technology of foolishness" as a way of advocating more playfulness in organizations. His article is worthy of careful investigation. Coming from what would now be considered a modernist perspective, March was still critical of what he identified as an overemphasis on rationality in organizations. He described three fundamental tenets of theories of choice theory and decision making: the preexistence of purpose, the necessity of consistency, and the primacy of rationality (p. 330). Each of these, he believed, constrains organizational life. We posit that each, in excess, may also constrain authentic dialogue, as we have conceptualized it, and hence must be carefully assessed by educational leaders.

We have clearly demonstrated in earlier chapters that dialogue is not teleological; it does not have a predetermined direction nor a specific anticipated outcome. Nevertheless, much of what actually occurs belies the stated goal (to educate all children equally, for example) and requires considerable imagination to be justified in rational, purposeful terms. In Urban High School, one might want to argue simply that the closing assembly is fun, that it gives students an opportunity to come together in a sense of shared community, and that it has value apart from the stated purpose of the school, which is to educate all children to similar high levels.

In like fashion, if instead of simply repeating the rules about fighting and discipline to Mrs. Davis, a school administrator takes the time to enter into dialogue, to understand her perspective and her situation, and to make connections with her as a distraught mother concerned for the welfare of her son, we might well applaud the effort. Here, too, encounter would have come not from a desire for efficiency, but from the conviction that having a meaningful encounter, treating the other with absolute regard, and engaging in dialogue are the right things to do.

On another occasion, it might well be important for the administrator, faced with a defiant student, to focus on the rules and consequences in order to ensure the safety of the school. Is this lack of consistency troubling? Some would argue that it is. We have been in many schools where one of the loudest complaints of teachers is that the principal does not apply the rules of discipline consistently. He or she, they claim, deals differently with different students. The complaint is based, as March suggests, on the second tenet of choice theory: the necessity of consistency.

We prefer the more playful approach suggested by Sidorkin and others. When one is totally consistent, one has stopped being open, stopped learning and growing. Consistency, we might therefore argue, is antithetical to dialogue. For how can one be consistent and open to change at the same time? Consistency is a quality of machines; we want and need them to operate in consistent fashion. Although there are times when consistency is desirable, we can push it too far. We do not want our human interactions to be machine-like, for such a quality inhibits dialogue. Acting with absolute consistency requires that we approach the other as an It, a subject, with nothing to teach us. Sidorkin (1999) writes:

> The self integrates around the need to remain open and unfinished, and around the purpose of dialogue with others.... The ideal of internal consistency of the self-concept may help destroy our dialogical potential. (p. 65)

Hence, the need for consistency can shut down our potential for inner dialogue or for moral dialogue (we might argue)—if you accept, as we do, that morality has a dialogical nature. We must constantly be reflecting on, and questioning, our choices, our actions, and our decisions in the light of who we are encountering at a given moment, their position, and their need, and in the light of benchmark criteria (such as those suggested in Chapter Four) that guide us toward educational communities that are socially just and academically excellent.

March (1976) identified the primacy of rationality as the third tenet of choice theory. When we take a rational approach, he claims, we examine the evidence, identify pros and cons, seek the choice that has the greatest congruence with our goals and values, and act accordingly. Yet, few of us would dispute the fact that we often act in ways contrary to what is sometimes overwhelming evidence; we act because something "feels right"; we use our "intuition" or simply choose an alternate course because the rational approach is not working. Inviting Sonny to come to my house instead of assigning one more detention was not rational teacher behaviour, but it worked. Inviting Michel to come to our graduate class seemed a rational choice, but it was fraught with other difficulties.

Given that the traditional, rational approaches to organizational life do not always "work," March (1976) offers an alternative. He argues that we need to "supplement the technology of reasons with a technology of foolishness [because] individuals and organizations need ways of doing things for which they have no good reason" (p. 335). He then proceeds to define playfulness as "the deliberate, temporary relaxation of rules in order to explore the possibilities of alternate rules" (p. 337). Play, conceived in this way, becomes an medium of intelligence, not an adversary of intelligent behavior. The Christmas assembly becomes an alternate form of education, a new way of looking at the school community, and not simply a waste of time.

Although March (1976) does not call his approach "carnival," it bears some resemblance to the notion of carnival that is one of Bakhtin's primary concepts. Bakhtin's early examination of carnival was contained in his doctoral dissertation, written about the work of Rabelais. Rabelais was a 16th century Franciscan monk who left the order to study medicine and to write books that are best known for their humorous and satirical condemnation of power and privilege. Often condemned as blasphemous, Rabelais' books were, for a while, banned both by academics and by the Church. For example, the entry about Rabelais in the *Catholic Encyclopedia* contains these words:

> He took pleasure in the worst obscenities. His vocabulary is rich and picturesque, but licentious and filthy. In short, as la Bruyère says: "His book is a riddle which may be considered inexplicable. Where it is bad, it is beyond the worst; it has the charm of the rabble; where it is good it is excellent and exquisite; it may be the daintiest of dishes." As a whole it exercises a baneful influence. (Cohen-Bacrie, 2001)

Bakhtin, however, did not see in Rabelais' work a licentious and filthy commentary on daily life, but rather one inspiration for his notion of carnival—a way of overthrowing the hierarchies and hypocrisy of the times and inviting everyone, regardless of role or station in life, to participate more fully and joyously. In later studies, Bakhtin elucidated the novel, and particularly the writings of Dostoevsky, to demonstrate how carnivalesque and polyphonic ways of looking at the world "permit the latent sides of human nature to be revealed and developed" (1973, p. 101).

Beyond Play: Carnival as Re-Creation

Interest in Bakhtin's concept of carnival as holding some interest for educators is not new. Toohey, Waterstons, and Julé-Lemke (2000) use the concept of carnival to examine classroom activities for non-English-speaking Punjabi and Sikh children. Others have used the concept of carnival to propose new pedagogical strategies for writing (see Chapman, 1999; Farmer, 1998; Swaim, 2002), for math education (van Oers, 2001), or to provide an alternative to experiential learning for adult learners (Michelson, 1999). Some have found in these concepts a way of rethinking parental involvement (Valle & Aponte, 2002) or bilingual education (Grutman, 1993). Yet the potential for dialogue and carnival to help us re-create our educational institutions and to revitalize educational leadership theory remains relatively unexplored.

While the Christmas skit and melodrama of Urban High School contain some playful, even carnivalesque elements, they fall short of the all-encompassing concept of carnival developed by Bakhtin. He describes carnival as a "pageant without a stage and without a division into performers and spectators" (1973, p. 3). He elaborates:

> In the carnival everyone is an active participant, everyone communes in the carnival act. Carnival is not contemplated, it is, strictly speaking, not even played out; its participants *live* in it...it is to a degree, "life turned inside out." (p. 100–101)

While the school plays tried to turn life inside out for a few moments, they were not, strictly speaking, events in which everyone participated actively. To be sure, there was the yelling and screaming typical of slapstick comedy or melodrama as all students booed the villains and cheered the heroes and heroines, but student participation was not complete.

In contrast, Bakhtin's notion of carnival is so uninhibited, so sensual, so "inside out and upside down" that, at first, it may appear to have little relevance to the ways in which educational leaders might think about their schools or to the concept of dialogue we have been so carefully developing. Because the concept is so radical, we propose to take a few minutes to explore Bakhtin's notion and then to come back to the question of its relevance for dialogic school leadership.

Carnival—A Fantastic Experiment

Bakhtin's interest in carnival is not merely because of its potential to bring some enjoyment to an otherwise "dull" life; rather, he sees it as a way of changing power structures, overthrowing hierarchies, suspending rules, and hence of creating the conditions under which dialogue is more likely to occur. Here, as we attempt to understand his meaning, we hold in the background a shared interest in carnival as a catalyst and facilitator of dialogue in educational settings.

Bakhtin (1973) explains:

> The laws, prohibitions and restrictions which determine the system and order of normal, i.e., non-carnival, life are for the period of carnival suspended;...i.e., everything that is determined by socio-hierarchical inequality among people or any form of inequality, including age. All *distance* between people is suspended and a special carnival category goes into effect—the *free, familiar contact among people*. (p. 100–101)

Carnival, therefore, may provide a hint of how to overcome some of the hegemonic differences that exist in institutions such as schools, organizations in which differences of age, responsibility, knowledge, formal educational and training, and hierarchical responsibilities are inherent. Although we have seen that, to some extent, these differences may be mitigated by the use of modesty and "absolute regard" in which we come into dialogue with another and let our differences fade into the background, there is no doubt that finding ways to suspend the differences even temporarily would also be helpful.

Bakhtin (1973) suggests that carnival emphasizes aspects of life normally suppressed or denied in both public and private life; it also provides the context within which differences may be overcome. When we enter into free and familiar contact with those whom we rarely approach, when we make use of "eccentricity" to "permit the latent sides of human nature to be revealed" (p. 101), when we form "carnivalistic mésalliances" which encompass "all values, thoughts, phenomena and things" (p. 101), and when we make use of profanation, "a carnivalistic system of lowering of status," we are turning the normal world "upside down" and creating an environment free of the usual constraints and barriers. The powerful become the powerless, the ruler becomes the ruled, the responsible become irresponsible, etc. Moreover, this does not occur in purely theoretical or abstract ways, but in real, material, embodied, and sensuous fashion as people are fully involved in the activities of the moment. When a school principal, for example, participates in a "dunk tank," shaves his head, or dyes her hair purple, the evidence of a changed reality is dramatic and concrete—available in the "public square" for all to behold.

Carnival, says Bakhtin (1973),

> is an attitude toward the world which liberates from fear, brings the world close to man and man close to his fellow man (all is drawn into the zone of liberated familiar contact), and, with its joy of change and its jolly relativity, counteracts the gloomy, one-sided official seriousness which is born of fear, is dogmatic and inimical to evolution and change, and seeks to absolutize the given conditions of existence and the social order. The carnival attitude liberated man from precisely this sort of seriousness. But there is not a grain of nihilism in carnival, nor, of course, a grain of shallow frivolity or trivial vulgar bohemian individualism. (p. 133)

Carnival, by its very nature, does not permit fear. Its laughter is genuine, not tinged with fear, but expansive and liberating. If the normal routines of the institution are dogmatic and inimical to change, carnival transforms them. Carnival is change and flexibility; it is the unanticipated, the unusual, the unexpected. It brings to the fore a new conception of space and time, of relationships and interactions.

When one thinks of carnivalistic moments in an educational setting, one thinks of whole school events: sports days; Christmas assemblies; dress-up days—in which administrators, teachers, and students all wear pyjamas, beach clothes, or period costumes; days when students take over the office and teachers attend class; multicultural fairs; or talent shows. But carnival occurs in pedagogical moments within classes as well. Consider the teacher who invites all students to pile onto a small square board, slightly raised from the floor, in a carnivalistic "encounter" in an attempt to create a sense of community (see McHenry [1997] for a description of this "All Aboard" activity as pedagogic carnival). Consider the physics teacher who asks his students to design mini-parachutes for raw eggs and takes his class to the flat roof of the school where the parachutes are launched and their "success" evaluated. What of the school that, instead of the usual formal and stodgy opening professional development day activities, enrolls the whole staff on a "ropes course" in which the goal is experience and encounter (in the way Buber used the term), rather than content-oriented planning. McHenry describes an approach to carnival in this way:

> What I envision here…[is] the prior possibility of establishing in a classroom an orientation of care wherein "speech in its ontological sense" springs from and reflects the presence of living persons facing each other. (p. 7)

This is exactly what Bakhtin's carnival brings to the forefront: the living presence of people facing each other, all barriers dropped, rules suspended, and power forgotten—at least for the moment. Note that Bakhtin (1973) insists carnival is not nihilism, not vulgar individualism, not shallow frivolity, but a joyous "sensuous, half-real, half-play acted form, a new modus of interrelationships of man with man which is counter-posed to the omnipotent hierarchical social relationships of non-carnivalistic life" (p. 101). Understood in this way, carnival establishes the conditions in which dialogic relations may more fully be understood and developed, in which new ways of relating are introduced and subsequently sustained.

Carnival: Dialogic Relationships

This description of carnival is enticing; it is all encompassing; it invites every member of the community to participate fully. It clothes the institution in the festive garb of human life in its unfettered fullness. Bakhtin (1973) sums up:

We have spoken of the characteristics of the structure of the carnival image: it strives to encompass and unite within itself both poles of evolution or both members of an antithesis: birth-death, youth-age, top-bottom, face-backside, praise-abuse, affirmation-negation, the tragical—the comical, etc. and the upper pole of a two-in-one image is reflected in the lower, after the manner of the figures on playing cards. It could be expressed thus: opposites meet, look at one another, are reflected in one another, know and understand one another. (p. 148)

In other words, carnival is polyphonic. It bears within it the totality of human existence, all perspectives, all emotions, all experiences. Thus, carnival is also fundamentally dialogic. We recall that Bakhtin (1973) believed that truth cannot be contained within a single voice or "reside in the head of an individual person; it is born of the dialogical intercourse between people in the collective search for truth" (p. 90). As all members of the community participate in carnivalesque behaviors, shedding their inhibitions, ignoring the established order and structures, all are liberated, able to come face to face with one another and into dialogic relation with another, expressing themselves fully without fear of censure or reprisal—for roles, rules, authority, and accountability are temporarily set aside. There is space for the collective search for truth, for all perspectives, all ideas, and all attitudes—regardless of how politically incorrect or how dangerous they might appear at another time. The inclusive and participatory nature of carnival highlights the polyphony of humanity, a polyphony that "is incompatible with the representation of a single idea executed in the ordinary way" (p. 63).

If educational leaders acknowledge that truth (with a small "t") cannot be contained within a single person or idea, then they must ensure that every member of the organization has an opportunity to participate. It is not simply a matter of democracy, but of understanding, in deeper and more meaningful ways, the needs of the membership and of learning ways in which to effect change to better respond to people's needs.

When Bakhtin (1973) summarizes the tensions of carnival, he uses another image of play: the figures on playing cards. Never fusing, never meeting, these figures represent the dialogic reality. Upside-down and facing in opposite directions, together they represent the reality of the game as we have come to know it. We look in one direction and "know" what the image is supposed to represent; turn the card around, and we still "know" because the images take meaning even in their opposition one to the other. Indeed, this is one way in which we come to know and understand, says Bakhtin:

Everything lives on the very border of its opposite. Love lives on the very border of hate, which it knows and understands, and hate lives on the border of love, and also understands it…. Faith lives on the very border of atheism, sees its reflection in atheism and understands it, and atheism lives on the border of faith and understands it…. (p. 148)

In a dialogic world, understanding, rather than conflict, is the primary outcome of a meeting between different objects or Subjects. We reflect and elucidate reality dialogically. If we think we know "everything" and have no room for doubt, no place for changing our opinion or making a different decision, we cannot engage in dialogue; we cannot live dialogically. When we express different perspectives in our speech utterances with another, we can be said to engage in dialogue.

Hence, carnival is one way to facilitate dialogue. It can change the structures, cultures, and realities just enough to permit those who have been marginalized to move to the center (however temporarily); it mutes those who have power and permits those who have been less dominant to speak. It mocks the rules of hierarchy and accountability, turning them on their heads, and, in their place, invites others to join the dance. It overcomes our self-consciousness, the closedness of our realities, and opens us to one another in the new modus of interrelationships.

Carnival: Educational Leadership with a Difference

If carnival is one way of changing the context, overcoming some of the organizational structures and hierarchical power differences that act as barriers to genuine dialogue, then what can an educational leader do to create the conditions for carnival that may permit dialogue to flourish?

We start with the need to take seriously the experiential, the need for learning (whether on the part of teachers or students) to authentically combine relationships and understanding, thought and action, cognition and emotion. Michelson (1999) believes these notions, found in Bakhtin's description of carnival with its emphasis on the experiential, embodied self, provide the basis for a new way of thinking about adult education. She writes, "Viewed most broadly, the promise of experience is the promise of a realm of authentic life—thought and feeling, action and interaction, the construction of the usable, sharable truths and imagination and play" (p. 4). We posit that this is equally true for the education of children.

In the article mentioned earlier, *The Technology of Foolishness*, March (1976) argued that in Western societies we have developed two parallel theories of reality: one for adults and one for children. Children are permitted to "play" because we adults believe it fosters choices that lead to "experiences that develop the child's scope, his complexity, his awareness of the world" (p. 333). March urges us to consider that:

> Individuals and organizations need ways of doing things for which they have no good reason. Not always. Not usually. But sometimes. They need to act before they think. (p. 335)

His words contain shadowy overtones of modernism, with its emphasis on rationality, technicality, and linear thinking. But in them, we also find echoes of postmodernism, the carnivalesque, the nonrational. Moreover, the advice rings true. Carnival is not a permanent state of affairs, but occurs at various times throughout the year. Its importance however, is difficult to overestimate. Sidorkin (1997) describes the spring *sbor*, an annual event in which all adults and children from a small school in Moscow spend three intense days together, engaged in skit-making, sports, and games, but primarily simply building a sense of community. He writes:

> Carnival has profound impact on the social organization of the school. Karakovskii's sbor takes less than one percent of the year, but it is undeniably the most important event of the school year. It energizes the whole school community and brings about a peculiar feeling of liberation and connectedness. The sbor symbolizes everything dear to the school community; it has a power to cancel troubles, smooth conflicts, and put everything into perspective. (p. 6)

While one cannot prescribe or even anticipate what will occur during carnival, the celebration itself is anticipated, even planned; it does not occur spontaneously. The *sbor* is carefully planned on an annual basis; medieval carnival was in fact scheduled as a "phenomenon of pre-Lenten, Shrovetide, or Mardi-Gras" (Bakhtin, 1973, p. 88)—a time of particular jollity and festivity that preceded the solemnity of the Lenten and Easter periods in the Christian Church. Planning for carnival to occur and prescribing what is to occur are therefore two different things. The educational leader may well need to take responsibility for the former, but the latter (planning the occurrence) must be left to fullness of the carnivalistic attitude with its "indestructible vivacity and the mighty, life-giving power to transform" (Bakhtin, 1973, p. 88).

When the educational leader sets out to plan for carnival, the "rules" for "sensible foolishness" developed by March may be of some use. Likewise, the less "functional," more chaotic tenets of carnival as outlined by Rabelais and described by Bakhtin may also offer some useful insights.

March (1976) suggests that we ought to treat "goals as hypotheses...intuition as real...hypocrisy as a transition...memory as an enemy...and experience as a theory" (p. 339). He explains each in turn in some detail; here we will simply paraphrase his key ideas. In general, he is arguing for ways to experiment with new ideas, including alternate goals, to defer (or eliminate) the need to justify every decision and every act in rational ways. We need to recognize that because we are always in flux, always learning, what we sometimes decry as hypocrisy may actually be a time of transition when it is difficult to articulate new perspectives, a time when we are experiencing change, experimenting with new ideas and approaches, trying them on for size. Memory becomes an enemy when it forces us to remain closed, when it protests, "but we've always done it this way...." It keeps us closed to new possibilities, to understanding the Other with whom we come in contact. "We tried that and it did not work....; we did it that way in a different organization, but it failed...." and so forth. Memory truly is an enemy if it prevents us from recognizing the uniqueness of each new situation and from acting in new and creative ways.

Although he does not use Bakhtin's terms, March (1976) is in fact arguing for a dialogic rather than a monologic approach to organizational life—keeping our options open, listening to alternative perspectives, learning from them, and incorporating new ideas into the fabric of our being. Relying on past performance, prior knowledge, and our own rational thinking does not lead, he suggests, to developing "the unusual combinations of attitudes and behaviors that describe the interesting people, interesting organizations, and interesting societies of the world" (p. 314). Perhaps more importantly for our purposes, it does not lead to the meaningful new relationships or deeper understandings necessary for living in community with those who are in some ways "different" from ourselves.

March's "rules" for playfulness certainly provide a place to start for the educational leader wanting to create the conditions under which dialogue may flourish. Helping people break out of prior habits and become open to new ways of thinking and acting will certainly facilitate dialogue; yet, in and of themselves, the rules do not go far enough. In his early excursion into the literary world of Rabelais, Bakhtin (1984) developed many of the ideas about carnival that he expanded in his later study of Dostoevsky. He consistently reminds us that carnival "is not a spectacle seen by the people; they live in it" (p. 7). Moreover, he asserts:

> Carnival celebrated temporary liberation from the prevailing truth and from the established order; it marked the suspension of all hierarchical rank, privileges, norms, and prohibitions. Carnival was the true feast of time, the feast of becoming, change, and renewal. (p. 10)

In carnival, communication that is impossible at other times is made possible; interactions that are prohibited at other times are permitted; new forms of speech and relationships that are constrained at other times are freed from restrictions; fear is replaced by bold optimism. Creation and re-creation are made possible, in part, by the norms of carnival.

Carnival[1] is characterized, according to Bakhtin (1984), by full participation, the use of humor, challenges to existing hierarchical relationships, the use of masks (that enable us to present multiple persona and to overcome fear), new forms of communication, empowerment, and the re-creation of boundaries. New structures, relationships, and patterns of communication rise from the old forms of institutional life through innovative ways of being that help people to see alternatives of possibility and justice.

Educational leaders who want to use more carnivalesque approaches to encourage dialogue will want to pay particular attention to encouraging these characteristics in their schools in ways that foster deeper relationships and understandings. One can see how the Christmas assembly introduced at the outset of this chapter is but one small illustration of possible carnivalesque behaviors and attitudes. The humor was a way of celebrating some of the events of the past term, poking gentle fun at the well-known quirks of individuals, a particular saying of a favorite teacher, the rallying cry of the student council president, and so forth. "Masks" and new identities were introduced. The student council secretary became the vice-principal, the principal became the villain, the typing teacher became the heroine, the student who was known to be struggling and often truant became one of the heroes, and so forth. These were not the masks of fear, shame, or protection we sometimes put on to prevent us from knowing and being known, but

---

[1]   For a discussion of these points, see Shields (2003), p. 196–208. Chapter 7 of this work both elaborates the characteristics and gives some examples and illustrations from schooling.

rather the joyous and playful masks of carnival. Students became technicians, teachers their assistants; students and teachers become playwrights, actors, and musicians. Each becomes the other as he or she mimics the dress, speech, and gestures of the character to be represented.

One can easily think of other examples of carnival that sometimes exist within schools. We know of one school in which, to start their professional development day, the staff play a game of mini-golf in the halls. In another, an annual water-fight breaks out; staff and students alike bring their weapons to school during the spring, hiding them until "the right moment"; there is no announcement, but at a propitious moment the battle is enjoined. There are no teams and no rules, but all participate for this one occasion when rules are suspended and the fun interrupts the routine.

Sometimes carnival occurs within the structures and walls of a school or classroom; at other times, it occurs because an event is scheduled beyond the physical confines of the institution. Staff retreats, student camps, field trips, athletic meets, coaching, highway cleanup day—all can act as catalysts for new patterns of communication, for seeing one another in different roles and in a different light. The teacher with so much content expertise in the chemistry classroom may be inept at rock climbing and need the help of her students to scale the wall. The student at the top of the honor role is taught how to light a campfire and prepare a meal by one who struggles in the senior French class; members of the football and basketball teams chide the English teacher for his slower hiking pace, and ultimately one offers to carry the gear of an older teacher who seems to be lagging behind. In each case, the conditions are established that change hierarchies and predicted modes of relating and communicating and establish new ones based on regard for the other person. Too often in institutions, we focus on a single aspect of what someone knows or can do, ignoring the rest of the person's achievements, accomplishments, and interests.

Carnival permits us to know the other in a slightly different way. It is difficult for the teacher and students who hiked, climbed, camped, or cooked together to maintain authoritarian barriers when back in the classroom. A dialogic, participatory orientation to one another has occurred, and in some small ways, their lives have been changed. "People who are in life separated by impenetrable hierarchical barriers enter into free, familiar contact on the carnival sphere" (Bakhtin, 1973, p. 101).

Dialogic Moments: Creating and Re-Creating

We have been exploring ways in which playfulness and carnival may help to get beyond some of the constraints of traditional institutional life. We have argued that even when educators attempt to live dialogically, there are sometimes barriers of power, hierarchy, roles, and communication that constrain dialogue and make living dialogically more difficult. Nevertheless, we believe that the possibilities inherent in creating deeply democratic school communities in which people live and work in relationship and understanding with one another are so significant that they are worth the effort to learn how to relate to one another in creative new ways. For that reason, this chapter has focused on how to break down some of the barriers, suspend some of the rules and norms, and live more freely, joyously, even somewhat impudently in carnivalesque modes.

It is important to note, however, that even when we temporarily suspend the routines of daily living, the criteria we introduced in Chapter Four cannot be suspended. We cannot act, either in carnival or in more routine times, in ways that contravene our concepts of justice, democracy, empathy, and optimism. Indeed, the very opposite is the case. Carnival, in its rejection of the prohibitions and restrictions that too often govern our institutional life, permits us to be more just, democratic, empathic, and optimistic.

Can we use these criteria as lenses to assess each and every activity that occurs within a school or to guide every decision that might be made? The answer, it seems, may be a tentative, "Well, yes and no." While it may be difficult to fathom how one could determine whether the Christmas assembly was, at its core, just, democratic, empathic, and optimistic, we could certainly identify ways in which it might disregard these criteria. If the melodrama singled out specific students or groups of students for ridicule, embarrassing and hurting them, rather than laughing, playing, and participating with them, it would be unjust and should not proceed. If only some students were permitted to attend the performance, it would not be democratic; moreover, if only the "in" group of teachers was permitted to participate, rather than it being a gift of the whole staff, it would be divisive rather than celebratory. If the theme of the melodrama was intended as a critique of existing practices or a criticism of the attitudes or behaviors of specific members of the community, then the joyous final day assembly might not be an appropriate venue for such issues to be raised. As it unfolded though, on an annual basis, the Christmas assembly provided a light, humorous, playful, and optimistic way for the term to end, for students to come together, ignoring who was popular, successful in athletics, high achieving academically—for none of this was the focus. Here the focus was on community building, on creating shared experiences that helped to weave together the fabric of the school community. Here, neither principal, nor vice-principal, nor student council president had particular power, but joined in a sort of carnival in which hierarchies were overturned and celebration ruled.

This is the message we take from carnival. If educational leaders are to build educational communities in which all members may participate freely in dialogic moments, they must not only engage in, but model, practice, and indeed, live dialogue. They must find ways to facilitate, encourage, foster, and create dialogue. They must intentionally open opportunities for significant encounters, new modes of interaction, and new opportunities for meaningful relationships. And they must do so in intentional ways.

Carnival and playfulness have the potential not only to make life in the school community more enjoyable, more interesting, and more engaging; they hold the promise of liberation, empowerment, freedom, understanding, and relationships. In other words, carnival is one approach to a new way of living, an ontology in which, in Bakhtin's (1973) words, "opposites meet, look at one another, are reflected in one another, know and understand one another" (p. 148). We need to find our voices and to hear those of others. We need to orient ourselves among the heteroglossia of competing voices and to stand in relation to them.

In order to accomplish this, educational leaders must renounce monologism and take up dialogic habits and approaches. We must become familiar with and comfortable in the complexity and ambiguity of polyphony. As Bakhtin (1973) states

> Dialog...is not the threshold to action, but the action itself. Nor is it a means of revealing, of exposing the already-formed character of a person; no, here the person is not only outwardly manifested, he becomes for the first time that which he is, not only—we repeat—as far as others are concerned, but for himself as well. To be means to communicate dialogically. When the dialog is finished, all is finished. Therefore the dialog, in essence, cannot and must not come to an end. (p. 213)

Perhaps the essence of being an educational leader is to ensure that the dialogue does not end, that attitudes and actions do not become fixed, dead, and deadly, but that the school community remains alive and vibrant, knowing others and helping them to be known, listening to others and helping them both to understand and be understood. For if the school does not provide the conditions under which its members may both be and be manifested to others, in which we may understand more deeply and know ourselves and others more fully, then it fails in its core educational mission.

CONCLUSION

A New Ground for Educational Leadership

We have presented a vision of dialogue and an approach to educational leadership that offers the possibilities of new ways of living together in schools, new ways of thinking about leading and learning. We have focused on the importance of remaining open to one another, meeting the Other with "absolute regard," and taking neither a relativistic nor a dogmatic approach to life, but a celebratory and integrated attitude. In previous chapters, we have developed the dialogic moment as a time of to-and-fro communication between two individuals whose open and respectful interactions help each to achieve deeper relationships and understandings. We have also argued that life in educational communities is, to a large extent, composed of a multiplicity of single dialogic moments, in which we come to appreciate and better understand those who are different from ourselves. We have developed some criteria for examining our interactions and have also suggested that, at times, a carnivalesque approach that sets aside the dominant rules and structures, at least temporarily, may facilitate the type of dialogue we have been describing.

Undergirding the whole book is the image of dialogue as ontological, as central to our being. Our concept of dialogue is graphically represented in Figure 4, a figure in which we represent relationships and understanding as ontologically grounded, with dialogue at the center. We have drawn inspiration from some of the great 20th century thinkers: Bakhtin, Buber, Freire, and Gadamer, as well as some more contemporary educators to develop our concept of dialogic leadership. Our concept of dialogue requires the educational leader to take on concepts that have not been central to leadership theories—risk, trust, openness to others, suspension of judgment, awareness of one's own biases and situatedness, and above all, a deeply moral and ethical stance.

Figure 4. The Ontological Dimension of Dialogue

Our vision of dialogue is one that empowers rather than deforms (as Freire put it). We believe that dialogue, like relationship and understanding, is fundamental to a fulfilling life; it requires and facilitates lifelong learning, constant openness to others, and continual growth and change on the part of individuals and ultimately the organizations of which they are a part. We conceptualize dialogue, not as an instrumental approach or strategy that permits the educational leader to acquire more knowledge to be used to predict and control behavior within the organization, not as a way of gaining information that permits one to hold power over another, but as a way of empowering all parties in the relational community.

We conceive of dialogue as deeply ontological and deeply pedagogical. It builds on the lived experiences of those who form the educational community, whether they are children or adults. It develops new understandings, new ways of living and being together in pluralistic societies. It engages adults and students together in deeply personal and meaningful ways in the shared activities of making meaning and of figuring out how best to act to balance the needs of individuals, subgroups, and the organization as a whole. When dialogue emanates from a desire to hold the other in absolute regard, it is eminently moral and ethical, grounding leadership practice in purposeful, moral, and ethical ways.

We are aware that our vision of dialogic leadership risks being dismissed as too idealistic and simultaneously too simplistic and too difficult. Yet we are convinced that it is not only possible, but perhaps the only way to exercise educational leadership in pluralistic school communities, the best way to avoid falling into the traps of mechanistic, managerial leadership, relativism, or dogmatism. We do not claim that anyone can live permanently or perfectly in dialogic relationships; nevertheless, we posit that unless educational leaders both understand and strive to attain the types of relationships and understanding made possible by dialogue, they are missing the most powerful way to foster the development of deeply democratic school communities so essential to education that is both equitable and excellent. We reiterate that our vision of dialogue is not simply talk, but relationships and understanding that lead to ethical action—action that is essential, communal, and collaborative.

We are constantly aware of the pluralism of our school communities, the rich and complex cultures, languages, backgrounds, perspectives, and preferences of those who come together. Sometimes we celebrate the differences, sometimes we are perplexed by them, and regularly we are challenged, as leaders, to know how to unite members of a richly diverse school community to act together in meaningful ways. Bakhtin (1973) commented:

> These voices are not self-enclosed and are not deaf to one another. They constantly hear each other, call out to one another, and are mutually reflected in one another....
> (p. 62)

We are convinced that dialogue, especially the multiplicity of dialogues that can occur regularly throughout an organization, really can make a difference. This is especially true when one member of the community approaches the other with absolute regard, permitting the establishment of an encounter in which words may become more than just talk.

Let us revisit the scenarios presented throughout this book and imagine they occurred in the context of dialogue.

*Well, Mrs. Davis, your son, David, has been caught fighting.... I
wonder if you could provide me with an insight into why a young
man with such an exemplary record might have lost his temper so
badly....*

or

*Sonny, I realize that you do not find French particularly interesting
or relevant. I wonder if you could tell me what your educational
hopes and goals are, and then we might be able to determine
together how you could reach them. You might need French, but then
again you might not. Can we talk?*

or

*Kenny. Something is not working for either of us in this situation.
You seem really unhappy in this class and I am frustrated because
your unhappiness is disruptive to others. I'd like to understand what
I can do to improve the situation. Can you tell me what is not
working for you?*

Each of the above openings is consistent with the image of dialogue we
have presented. There is nothing magical about them. They reflect
opportunities for deeper understanding, but have not yet moved into new
frameworks involving play or carnival. Further, even with these openings,
the responses of the others are certainly not predictable. One cannot be
certain that students will be able to trust educators enough to engage in
dialogue; there is no guarantee that the exchange thus engaged will be more
"successful" than the previous utterances, but there is definitely more
potential in these questions than in the dogmatic and emotional responses
previously presented.

One essential difference between these new utterances and those we
presented in earlier chapters is that here, in each instance, the educator has
acted with openness to the other, treating him or her with "absolute regard."
In these utterances, concern about the rules regarding fighting, undone
French homework, or a teacher's authority have been pushed into the
background, and interest in the individual has been placed front and center.
The educator has taken the time to *encounter* the Other as a Subject, a Thou,
rather than an "it." The focus is on *being* rather than *having,* on *relating to*
and *understanding a person* rather than solving a problem or resolving a
situation. In each situation, the educator has come, not with "content" but

with "presence." The educator stands ready to "be there" for the other, not judging, not imposing a position, but truly wanting to understand and to permit his or her new understanding to guide subsequent decisions and action. The educator stands in modesty and humility, acutely aware of the limits of her knowledge and her understanding. She is fully present to others, acknowledging her formal role and institutional authority, but conscious that the other's perspective also constitutes an essential part of the interaction.

In each of the above situations, the educator, by virtue of his or her situatedness, holds power over the other (principal over parent, teacher over student). Yet, when one encounters the other with openness, foregrounding one's prejudice and acknowledging what we have called "outsidedness," power relations can be moved into the background to make space for the other's voice. Outsidedness permits the educator to stand facing the parent or student, to delve deep inside his or her own self to discover the prejudices and biases that might be detrimental to the development of deeper relationships and understanding. It is possible that the educator may never come to agree with the other's perspective. Indeed, it is important that each educational leader be able both to *participate* with others, taking seriously what they need to say, but also to be able to stand firm, to hold her own ethical ground. The authentic leader must listen, hear, and understand with her mind, heart, and soul; paradoxically, she must also test new understandings and others' perspectives against her solid understanding of right and wrong, against the moral, ethical, and legal underpinnings of her formal position.

Bakhtin (1973) wrote:

> Only a dialogical, participatory orientation takes the word of another person seriously and approaches it as a semantic position, as another point of view. My word can maintain a close bond with the word of another, and at the same time not become one with it, not engulf it nor dissolve its significance.... (p. 52)

In making the choice for dialogue, the educator takes a risk. There is no guarantee that the other is ready to be open, wants to understand, or is willing to relate; but neither can the educator assume the opposite. There is no doubt that feelings run high in situations like these, yet we can, with effort, control our feelings. We can acknowledge that feelings are transitory, while relation is enduring; hence it is critical to recall Buber's insight that "feelings merely accompany the fact of the relationship which after all is established...between an I and a You" (1970, p. 129). When we realize that relationship is fundamental, ontological, and essential to what we are trying to do as educators, we must find ways to temper negative feelings in order to act with absolute regard for the other person.

When Dialogue Breaks Down....

We would be naïve if we did not admit that there are times when dialogue breaks down, times when it fails to deepen relationships and understanding. At times, when emotions run too high, we may need to initiate a cooling-off period. Sometimes we may simply need to show the other that we are open, but then to wait until he or she feels ready to take up the opportunity for dialogue. Sometimes, the readiness may not come and, sadly, we must walk away. Dialogue cannot be forced, coerced, or mandated. But even a slammed door does not necessarily mean that dialogue has not begun. Partial awareness may result from a sober second thought and prompt new ways of interacting during a subsequent encounter.

In Chapter Five, we recounted how we had introduced Michel to our class; we examined what we had done wrong and what we might have done differently, and we accepted responsibility for taking an approach that was predominantly monological, for failing to balance the needs of our students for both understanding and relationship. But that said, could we have ensured that no one would be upset, that Richard would not have been hurt?

We acknowledge that the potential and depths of dialogue that are possible are constrained by others' willingness to trust, to be open, to acknowledge that their knowledge is incomplete and that they need to know the other and his or her horizons. But dialogue may also be constrained by factors beyond the conscious awareness and control of any of the parties. Could we realistically expect Richard to set aside the years of loyalty to his father, years of helping him come to grips with being a Holocaust survivor, and to be immediately open to Michel's Palestinian perspective? Had we even been aware of Richard's historical embeddedness, could we have done anything to mitigate it? In reality, the space we created, although painful, may ultimately have created an opportunity for him to rethink his position. (He subsequently reported that his wife had told him he was overreacting and that he needed to be more open to other perspectives, and he commented that she might have been right.) Creating the conditions in which new voices—polyphony—can occur may not immediately facilitate open dialogue, but at the same time, may lead to a deep, ongoing, internal dialogue that ultimately will permit more openness at a future time.

What of a rape victim, a student whose parent has been on the front page of the local press for a heinous crime, or a parent who has been battered and abused and who has had to move her family to a local "safe house"? Our task is to hold the other in absolute regard, to be open, and to demonstrate consistently that we are trustworthy. But we must also respect the other's right "not to go there." Dialogical relationships are NOT counseling. We must not mistake being open for encouraging the other to "tell all." While there are times when having trust and a depth of relationship may provide the conditions under which one feels safe to share deeply, dialogue is not intended to be cartharsis. Indeed, in the educational setting, dialogue may more often and most properly be limited to those issues that have a bearing on the education of one's child or the children of the school community as a whole. Only in exceptional situations might the context of the dialogue stray well beyond the educational to the deeply personal.

Tevye in *Fiddler on the Roof* illustrates this point well. As a father who deeply loves his daughters but who also deeply honors his traditions, he has been able to agree to the marriages of his eldest two daughters into less-than-preferred situations, but when it comes to accepting his youngest daughter's determination to marry outside the tradition, he just cannot force himself to go there. This too is a position we must respect if we are relating to him with absolute regard. We must remember that on other occasions, despite his pain, he has been willing to listen and ultimately to come to a new point of action. This is the hope that causes us to persist with our concept of dialogic leadership. While there may be times when it does not "work," there will also be times of new insights, deeper relationships, and more innovative grounds for action.

Leading Dialogically in a Community of Difference

When we examine the vignettes of Hopeless High School, Hopeful High School, Mosaic Community School, and Urban High School, we find that they have much in common. In each school, educators strive to accomplish their goals; they care about the achievements of their students; they have tried innumerable programs, reforms, and new strategies to make a difference for their students. Yet, there is no doubt that there have been different degrees of "success" among the schools.

On the one hand, in both Hopeless High and Mosaic Community School, educators placed their trust and hope in new programs, putting time and energy into activities, but ignoring the fundamental need to encounter other members of the school community and to relate to them in I-Thou ways. The single-minded focus on objects, programs, and results was—and will always be—devoid of hope, empathy, and optimism because it ignores the ontological need for relationships. In Mosaic Community School, despite a realization that relationships were important, the attempts to forge them were still unsatisfactory in that the issue of power was never acknowledged, examined, or addressed. Teachers made decisions *for* the parents and students. There was no dialogue, no reciprocal understanding, no deeply democratic participation that permitted educators, parents, and students to come together in relationship and understanding to determine the directions of the school. In neither Hopeless High nor Mosaic Community School did we find dialogue based on criteria that might lead to a more socially just or academically excellent school. In fact, what we found most prevalent in these schools was monologism, closedness, and a lack of to-and-fro play that could lead to fusing of horizons or deep understanding.

On the other hand, in both Hopeful High and Urban High, we found elements of playfulness, openness, and carnival. In these schools, educators were more concerned with developing relationships, gaining reciprocal understanding, overcoming hierarchies, and establishing norms of community that would be just, democratic, empathic, and optimistic. Openness, encounter, and presence were combined with polyphony, heteroglossia, playfulness, and regard for others. A multiplicity of valid perspectives was acknowledged, many voices were heard, and new meanings were created. Learning occurred in meaningful ways, and individuals and groups came into new relationships with one another. The monologism of the previous schools was replaced by dialogism, by an emphasis on people rather than rules, and by an emphasis on understanding rather than on predetermined directions and anticipated right answers.

To some extent, Buber's (1970) description of what happens when one lives in relationship explains the differences in the various schools. He wrote:

> In the pure relationship you felt altogether dependent, as you could never possibly feel in any other—and yet also altogether free as never and nowhere else; created—and creative. You no longer felt the one, limited by the other; you felt both without bounds, both at once. (p. 130)

This is the key, we believe, to dialogic educational leadership. One can feel paradoxically and simultaneously entirely dependent and absolutely free. One feels dependent on the wisdom, support, and caring of the other with whom one has entered into understanding and relationship; yet, one is free to be fully alive, fully oneself. There is no need to take on masks or behaviors that hide your deepest realities because you have been encountered with absolute regard. The student feels free to learn, to explore, and to create because of the relationship he or she has forged with a teacher. The principal feels free to learn, to grow, to lead, and to create—a school community that is both socially just and academically excellent, both accountable and independent—because of the relationships with teachers, parents, and students that have been fostered over time and that ground his practice. The principal is free to act because of the relationships and understandings that have developed in which he has found his own voice and identity in the encounter with others. Out of the new learning comes action grounded in a deep and moral understanding of the community.

The educational leader who chooses to ground his or her leadership practice—the moral and deliberate interventions of daily life—in dialogue will soon find that it permeates and changes every aspect of the job. It becomes a scaffolding for interactions, for talking with teachers about curriculum and classroom management, for guiding committee deliberations, for working through conflict, and for making decisions. School goals and new policies will be developed through dialogic processes that ensure that each person has had an opportunity to share in a climate of trust, openness, and respect.

Practices related to teacher supervision can no longer be "top down," with the principal providing the teacher with one-way feedback in the form of a required checklist and summary statement. Instead, principal and teacher together will discuss the nature and context of the lesson, the challenges the teacher perceived, what was intended, who was well-served by a given approach, and how a lesson might be improved. Within a climate of dialogue and respect, principal and teachers work, not in oppositional and resentful ways, but together, to improve the classroom pedagogy for the good of all students.

In like fashion, decisions about things such as resource allocation, scheduling, and adoption of new programs, will be considered through dialogue, by the community as a whole. All perspectives will be heard, yet with the recognition that decisions can rarely, if ever, accommodate all perspectives. Nevertheless, participation in the dialogue will permit all members of the community to understand the reasons for a given decision, knowing that their perspective has also been carefully considered.

Conflict results when everyone is encouraged to express an opinion. Understanding results when each opinion is carefully considered, when each participant is treated with absolute regard and leaves knowing that he or she has contributed to the play of significance, to the polyphony of the communal process. The process is so profound that Palmer (1998) refers to the community that results as a *community of truth*. Teachers, students, parents, staff, community members, administrators all become educational leaders, each voice contributing to the creation of a community of difference, a community of respect and truth in which a focus on understanding and relationships guides all activities and decisions.

Palmer (1998) explains beautifully the role of conflict in a dialogic process. He writes:

> We enter into complex patterns of communication—sharing observations and interpretations, correcting and complementing each other, torn by conflict in this moment and joined by consensus in the next. The community of truth, far from being linear and static and hierarchical, is circular, interactive, and dynamic. (p. 103)

At its best, the community of truth advances our knowledge through conflict, not competition. Competition is a secretive, zero-sum game played by individuals for private gain; conflict is open and sometimes raucous but always communal, a public encounter in which it is possible for everyone to win by learning and growing.

No Final Word ...

We have seen previously that both Bakhtin and Gadamer assert the continuous, open-ended quality of dialogue. Bakhtin (1973) was particularly unequivocal; he wrote:

> When the dialogue is finished, all is finished. Therefore the dialog, in essence, cannot and must not come to an end. (p. 213)

What would it mean for the dialogue never to come to an end? What would it mean for the school administrator to develop in teachers and students an expectation of entering into dialogue? What would it mean for each member of the community to interact knowing that each encounter is the beginning of an ongoing dialogue, that each to-and-fro communication lays the basis for subsequent encounters? What kind of presence would we bring to our work if we truly understood that each word, each utterance, each encounter lays the groundwork for ongoing, deeper understanding and relationships in the future and that no word or act represents an unequivocal conclusion? Dialogism requires that we take action knowing that there is a "tomorrow" and that what happens today creates a basis for what happens tomorrow. The activities and utterances of each person, each day, become part of the rich fabric of school life.

What would it mean for the diverse members of a community of difference to live dialogically, continually developing new relationships and deeper understandings, and engaging in creative and re-creative acts that permitted new learning to occur in the contexts of justice and excellence? Bakhtin (1973) provides a hint. To enter into dialogic relations in a community, one's goal must be

> to find one's own voice and to orient it among other voices, to combine it with some of them and to counterpose it to others, or to separate one's voice from another voice, with which it is inseparably merged .... (p. 201)

This is the task to which educational leaders who are intent on leading dialogically are called. They will need to find their own voice, acknowledging their own biases and prejudices and their own historical and cultural situatedness. Then they will need to listen carefully in order to orient their voices among other voices. They must listen to others, hear them, relate to them, and understand them. The task then is to make some determinations of where one stands, of what one's own truths are, what can be negotiated, compromised, or merged, and where one must delineate boundaries.

But the task goes beyond the personal quest of the educational leader. The leader must help all members of the school community to find their voices and to orient them among all other voices. Amidst the heteroglossia of diverse perspectives, sounds, attitudes, ideas, and individuals, each person must be permitted to be fully *present*, to *encounter* and be encountered with absolute regard. Each person must learn when to combine his or her voice with that of another, when to counterpose it, and when to separate it.

In order to stand together, we must stand apart (as Gibran's temple pillars), finding our own voice amid the heteroglossia. Yet, paradoxically, it is in standing apart that we also come to know, to understand, and to relate to others. We meet at the boundaries of our understanding, our horizons, our trust, bringing our own self-awareness, our beliefs, and our ethical ground to the dialogue, opening ourselves to the possibility of new insights, new awareness, even to the possibility of change. Our separate voices become integrated into the warp and woof of school life, the glorious and exquisitely textured fabric of the school community.

As we have demonstrated throughout this book, the most important considerations for educational leaders are not those traditionally thought of: establish the boundaries of role; understand hierarchy, power, and position; select new programs, policies, and organizational structures; or solve problems quickly—put out fires! Rather, educational leadership works best when it is firmly grounded in dialogue, on an understanding of its ontological qualities that are inherently relational and that focus on understanding, not prescription. As educational leaders, we must first and foremost focus on knowing ourselves. Then, conscious of our own voice—sometimes muting it temporarily in order to hear others, sometimes silencing it altogether to set aside our positional authority and formal knowledge, we come more fully into dialogical relationship with those who live and work in our organizations. But sometimes, too, we must speak loudly and eloquently and share our insights, our understandings, and our wisdom for the good of the community. Being a dialogic leader does not require losing oneself, but finding oneself in the richness of the polyphonic community.

We are not advocating an approach to leadership that is neat, quick, or easy. We have not attempted to identify characteristics, traits, skills, or knowledge that will permit a leader to be more successful. Instead, we have argued for the simplest, and simultaneously the most difficult, way of thinking about educational leadership.

Know yourself and treat the other with absolute regard. Live openly and creatively on the borders of your comfort level and your understanding. Live dialogically—for this is the new ground for educational leadership.

The history of dialogical leadership has yet to be written, but in our own practice, we strive to set these ideas at the core of our daily lives, to use them to ground our leadership practice. We invite you to do the same. Together we will move forward, recognizing that life in our organizations is fundamentally a great dialogue. We can both rejoice and relax in this truth; for with Bakhtin (1973), we acknowledge that:

The final word of the world and about the world has not yet been said, the world is open and free, everything is still in the future and will always be in the future. (p. 138)

We do not need to solve all problems, to introduce all reforms, or to try every new program, for more horizons and landscapes will continue to present themselves to our awareness. But we do need to engage in dialogue, to live in dialogue, openly and freely. For that is how we can best exercise leadership in the education of all children within our society and how we can best encourage others to participate in the awesome dialogue of life and learning of which we are privileged to be a part.

REFERENCES

Argan. G. C. (1955). Found under "empathy": *Fra Angelico and his times*. Retrieved June, 2003, from http://www.artlex.com/ArtLex/E.html

Bacon, F. (1620/1960). *The new organon*. Indianapolis, IN: Bobbs-Merrill Educational Publishing.

Bakhtin, M. (1973). *Problems of Dostoevsky's poetics*. Ann Arbor, MI: Ardis.

Bakhtin, M. (1984). *Rabelais and his world*. (H. Iswolsky, Trans.). Bloomington, IN: Indiana University Press.

Bakhtin, M. M. (1986a). From notes made in 1970–71. (V. W. Mcgee, Trans.). In C. Emerson & M. Holquist (Eds.), *Speech genres and other late essays*. Austin, University of Texas Press. pp. 132–158.

Bakhtin, M. M. (1986b). Response to a question from the Novy Mir editorial staff. In C. Emerson & M. Holquist (Eds.), M. Holquist (Trans.), *Speech genres and other late essays*. Austin, TX: University of Texas Press. pp. 1–9.

Bakhtin, M. M. (1986c). The problem of speech genres. (V. W. Mcgee, Trans.). In C. Emerson & M. Holquist (Eds.), *Speech genres and other late essays*. Austin, University of Texas Press. pp. 60–102.

Bakhtin, M. M. (1986d). The problem of the text. (V. W. Mcgee, Trans.). In C. Emerson & M. Holquist (Eds.), *Speech genres and other late essays*. Austin, University of Texas Press. pp. 103–131.

Bakhtin, M. M., & Volosinov, V. N. (1973). *Marxism and the philosophy of language*. London: Harvard University Press.

Banks, J. A. (1991). Multicultural education: For freedom's sake. *Educational Leadership, 49*(4), pp. 32–36.

Barth, R. S. (1990). *Improving schools from within*. San Francisco, Jossey-Bass.

Beck, L., & Murphy, J. (1994). *Ethics in educational leadership programs: An expanding role*. Thousand Oaks, CA: Corwin.

Bellah, R. N., Madsen, R. D., Sullivan, W. M., Swindler A., & Tipton S. M. (1985). *Habits of the heart*. Los Angeles, University of California Press.

Bogotch, I. E. (2000). *Educational leadership and social justice: Theory into practice*. Revised version of a paper presented at the annual conference of the University Council for Educational Administration, Albuquerque, NM. ED 452 585.

Bohm, D. (1996). *On dialogue*. London: Routledge.

Bolman, L. G., & Deal, T. E. (1991). Everyday epistemology in school leadership: Patterns and prospects. In P. Hallinger, K. Leithwood, & J. Murphy (Eds), *Cognitive perspectives on educational leadership*. New York: Teachers College Press. pp. 21–33.

Borrowman, M. L. (1956). *The liberal and technical in teacher education*. New York: Teachers College Press.

Bourdieu, P., with Passeron, J.-C. (1977). *Reproduction in education, society and culture*. London: Sage.

Brookover, W. B., Beady, C., Flood, P., Schweitzer, J., Schneider, R., & Wisenbaker, J. (1979). *School social systems and student achievement: Schools can make a difference*. New York: Praeger.

Bryck, A. S. (1988). Musings on the moral life of schools. *American Journal of Education, 96*(2), pp. 256–290.

Buber, M. (1953). *I and Thou* (R. G. Smith, Trans.). New York: Charles Scribner & Sons.

Buber, M. (1970). *I and Thou*. (W. Kaufman, Trans). New York: Charles Scribner & Sons.

Buber, M. (1988). *The knowledge of man*. Atlantic Highlands, NJ: Humanities Press International.

Burbules, N. C. (1993). *Dialogue in teaching*. New York: Teachers College Press.

Chapman, M. L. (1999). Situated, social, active: Rewriting genre in the elementary classroom. *Written Communication, 16*(4), pp. 469–90.

Christie, J. F. (1980). The cognitive significance of children's play: A review of selected research. *Journal of Education, 162*(4), pp. 23–33, EJ 243330

Clark, D., Lotto, L. S., & Astuto, T. A. (1984). Effective schools and school improvement: A comparative analysis of two lines of inquiry. *Educational Administration Quarterly, 20*(3), pp. 41–68.

Cohen-Bacrie, P. (2001). *Rabelais*. Retrieved August 17, 2003 from http://pages.globetrotter.net/ pcbcr/rabelais.html

Colclough, C. (1993). Primary schooling in developing countries: The unfinished business. In T. &. B. C. Allsop (Eds.), *Oxford studies in comparative education*, Wallingford, Oxfordshire, UK: Triangle. pp. 47–58.

Culbertson, J. A. (1988). A century's quest for a knowledge base. In N. J. Boyan (Ed.), *Handbook of research on educational administration*, New York: Longman, pp. 3–26.

Culbertson, J. A. (1995). *Building bridges: UCEA's first two decades*. University Park, PA: UCEA.

Cutright, M. (2001). Introduction: Metaphor, chaos theory, and this book. In M. Cutright (Ed.), *Chaos theory and higher education*. New York: Peter Lang.

Dansky, J. L., & Silverman, I. W. (1977). Play: A general facilitator of associative fluency. *Developmental Psychology, 11*, p. 104.

Delpit, L. D. (1988). The silenced dialogue: Power and pedagogy in educating other people's children. *Harvard Educational Review, 58*(3), pp. 280–298.

Donmoyer, R. (1999). The continuing quest for a knowledge base: 1976–1998. In J. Murphy & K. S. Louis (Eds.). *Handbook of research on educational administration*, 2nd edition. San Francisco, Jossey-Bass, pp. 25–43.

Dorland's Illustrated Medical Dictionary. (2003). Retrieved August 20, 2003, from www.mercksource.com/pp/us/cns/cns_sign_in.jsp.

Dufour, R. (2001). How to launch a community: A new school principal talks openly about the challenges and benefits of creating a professional learning community. *Journal of Staff Development, 22*(3), pp. 50–51

Edwards, M., & Shields, C. M. (2002, May). *Dialogic leadership: Promise or fad?* Paper presented at the annual conference of the Canadian Association for Studies in Educational Administration, Toronto, Ontario.

Einstein, A. (1931). Speech to the California Institute of Technology as reported in the *New York Times*, February 17, 1931, p. 6. In S. Platt (Ed.), *Respectfully quoted*, New York: Barnes & Noble. p. 312.

English, F. W. (2003). *The postmodern challenge to the theory and practice of educational administration.* Springfield, IL: Charles C Tomas.

Erickson, E. H. (1950). *Childhood and society.* New York: Norton.

Etzioni, A. (1993). *The spirit of community.* New York: Touchstone.

Farmer, F. (1998). Dialogue and critique: Bakhtin and the cultural studies writing classroom. *College Composition and Communication, 49*(2), pp. 186–207.

Farrell, J. P. (1999). Changing conceptions of equality of education: Forty years of comparative evidence. In R. F. Arnove & C.A. Torres (Eds.), *Comparative education: The dialectic of the global and the local,* Lanham, MD: Rowman & Littlefield, pp. 149–177.

Fayol, H. (1997). General principles of management. In D. S. Pugh (Ed.), *Organization theory.* Toronto: Penguin. Pp. 63–67 (Original work published 1916.)

Follett, M. P. (2000). *The new state.* Retrieved August 16, 2003, from http://sunsite.utk.edu/FINS/Mary_Parker_Follett/Fins-MPF-01.html (Original work published 1918.)

Foster, W. (1986). Paradigms and promises: New approaches to educational administration. Buffalo, NY: Prometheus.

Foster, W. (1989). Toward a critical practice of leadership. In J. Smyth (ed.), *Critical perspectives on educational leadership.* London: Falmer. pp. 39–62.

Foucault, M. (1995). *Discipline and punish: The birth of the prison.* (A. Sheridan, Trans.). New York: Vintage Books.

Foucault, M. (2000). The subject and power. In J. D. Faubion & P. Rabinow (Eds.), *Michel Foucault: Power,* New York: The New Press, pp. 326–348.

Freire, P. (1983). *Pedagogy of the oppressed.* (M. B. Ramos, Trans.). New York: Continuum.

Freire, P. (2000a). Education for critical consciousness. In A. M. A. Freire & D. Macedo (Eds). *The Paulo Freire reader.* New York: Continuum, pp. 80–110.

Freire, P. (2000b). Learning to question: A pedagogy of liberation. In A. M. A. Freire & D. Macedo (Eds). *The Paulo Freire reader.* New York: Continuum, pp. 186–230.

Freire, P. (2000c). Pedagogy of hope: Reliving Pedagogy of the oppressed. In A. M. A. Freire & D. Macedo (Eds). *The Paulo Freire reader.* New York: Continuum, pp. 237–264.

Freire, P. (2000d). Pedagogy of the city. In A. M. A. Freire & D. Macedo (Eds). *The Paulo Freire reader.* New York: Continuum, pp. 231–236.

Freire, P. (2000e). Pedagogy of the oppressed, In A. M. A. Freire & D. Macedo (Eds). *The Paulo Freire reader*. New York: Continuum, pp. 45–79.

Freire, P. (2000f). Reading the word and the world. In A. M. A. Freire & D. Macedo (Eds). *The Paulo Freire reader*. New York: Continuum, pp. 163–185.

Fromm, E. H. (1994). *Escape from freedom*. New York: Henry Holt & Co.

Furman, G. C. (1998). Postmodernism and community in schools: Unraveling the paradox. *Educational Administration Quarterly. 34*(3), pp. 298–328.

Furman-Brown, G. (Ed.). (2002). *School as community: From promise to practice*. Albany, State University of New York Press.

Gadamer, H. G. (2002). *Truth and method*. (2nd ed.). (J. Weinsheimer & D. Marshall, Trans.). New York: Continuum.

Garber, D. (1998). Descartes, or the cultivation of the intellect. In A. O. Rorty (Ed.), *Philosophers on education*. London: Routledge, pp. 124–138.

Gibran, K. (1923). *The prophet*. Retrieved December 26, 2004, from www.columbia.edu/~gm84/ gibtable.html

Gilligan, C. (1982). *In a different voice: Psychological theory and women's development*. Cambridge, MA: Harvard University Press.

Glidewell, J. C. (1991). How CEOs change their minds. In P. Hallinger, K. Leithwood, & J. Murphy (Eds), *Cognitive perspectives on educational leadership*. New York: Teachers College Press. pp. 34–53.

Good, T., & Brophy, J. (1985). School effects. In M. C. Wittrock (Ed.), *Handbook of research on teaching* (3rd ed.), New York: Macmillan. pp. 570–602.

Goodlad, S. J. (2001). *The last best hope: A democracy reader*. San Francisco: Jossey-Bass.

Green, J. M. (1999). *Deep democracy: Diversity, community, and transformation*. Lanham, MD: Rowman & Littlefield.

Greenfield, T., & Ribbins, P. (1993). *Greenfield on educational administration*. New York: Routledge.

Griffeths, D. E. (1979). Intellectual turmoil in educational administration. *Educational Administration Quarterly, 13*(3), pp. 43–65.

Grumet, M. R., (1995). The curriculum: What are the basics and are we teaching them? In J. L. Kincheloe & S. R. Steinberg (Eds.), *Thirteen questions,* 2nd ed., New York: Peter Lang. pp.15–21.

Grutman, R. (1993). Mono versus stereo: Bilingualism's double face. *Visible Language, 27*(1-2), pp. 206–227.

Hallinger, P., Leithwood, K., & Murphy, J. (1991). Introduction. In P. Hallinger, K. Leithwood, & J. Murphy (Eds.), *Cognitive perspectives on educational leadership*. New York: Teachers College Press.

Halpin, A. W. (Ed.). (1958). *Administrative theory in education*. Chicago: The Midwest Center, University of Chicago.

Heraclitus. The Internet Encyclopedia of Philosophy. (2002), Retrieved August 22, 2003 from http://www.utm.edu/research/iep/h/ heraclit.htm

Hoy, W. (1994). *Introduction: Essential knowledge for school leaders*. Primis, NY: McGraw-Hill.

Jeans, J. (1942). *Physics and philosophy*. Cambridge: Cambridge University Press.

Kanpol, B., Yeo, F. (2000). Series forward. In M. L. Buley-Meissner, M. M. Thompson, E. B. Tan (Eds.). *The academy and the possibility of belief: Essays on intellectual and spiritual life*. Cresskill, NJ: Hampton Press. pp. ix–xii.

Kierstead, F. D., & P. A. Wagner, Jr. (1993). *The ethical, legal, and multicultural foundations of teaching*. Madison, WI: Brown & Benchmark.

Kincheloe, J., & Steinberg, S. (1995). The more questions we ask, the more questions we ask. In J. L. Kincheloe & S. R. Steinberg (Eds.), *Thirteen questions*, 2nd ed., New York: Peter Lang. pp. 1–12.

Kohlberg, L. (1981). *The philosophy of moral development: Moral stages and the idea of justice*. (1st ed.). San Francisco: Harper & Row.

Lankshear, C. (2003). On having and being: The humanism of Erich Fromm. In C. Lankshear, M. L. Peters, & C. Olssen (Eds.), *Critical theory and the human condition: Past, present, and future* New York: Peter Lang, pp. 54–66.

Leithwood, K., & Steinbach, R. (1991). The relationship between variations in patterns of school leadership and group problem-solving processes. In P. Hallinger, K. Leithwood, & J. Murphy (Eds), *Cognitive perspectives on educational leadership*. New York: Teachers College Press, pp. 103–129.

Liston, D. D. (2001). *Joy as a metaphor of convergence: A phenomenological and aesthetic investigation of social and educational change*. Cresskill, NJ: Hampton Press.

Lorenz, E. N. (1993). *The essence of chaos*. London: UCL Press.

Louis, K. S. (1996). Putting teachers at the center of reform: Learning schools and professional communities. *NASSP Bulletin, 80*(580), p. 9.

March, J. G. (1990). The technology of foolishness. In D. S. Pugh (Ed). *Organization theory*. Toronto: Penguin. pp. 329–341. (original work published 1976).

Maxcy, S. J. (1995). *Democracy, chaos, and the new school order*. Thousand Oaks, CA: Corwin.

May, S. (2000, April). *Multiculturalism in the 21st century: Challenges and possibilities*. Paper presented at the annual meeting of the American Educational Research Association, New Orleans.

Mayo, E. (1997). Hawthorne and the Western Electric Company. In D. S. Pugh (Ed.), *Organization theory: Selected readings*, New York: Penguin, pp. 355–368. (Original work published 1949.)

McCleary, L. E., & Ogawa, R. (1989). The assessment center process for selecting school leaders. *School Organization, 9*(1), pp. 103–113.

McHenry, H. D. (1997). Education as encounter: Buber's pragmatic ontology. *Educational Theory, 47*(3), pp. 1–13.

Michelson, E. (1999). Carnival, paranoia, and experiential learning. *Studies in the Education of Adults, 31*(2), pp. 140–154.

Minnich, E. K. (1995). *The drama of diversity and democracy, higher education and American commitments*. Report to Association of American Colleges and Universities. Washington, DC: Ford Foundation.

Mintzberg, H. (1983). *Power in and around organizations*. Englewood Cliffs, NJ: Prentice-Hall.

Mitchell, C. (1999). Building learning communities in schools: The next generation or the impossible dream? *Interchange, 30*(3), pp. 283–303.

Morgan, G. (1997). *Images of organization.* Newbury Park, CA: Sage.

Murphy, J. (1999). *The quest for a center: Notes on the state of the profession of educational leadership.* Columbia, MO: University Council for Educational Administration, UCEA Monograph series.

Murtadha-Watts, K. (1999). Spirited sisters: Spirituality and the activism of African American women in educational leadership. In L. Fenwick (Ed.), *School leadership: Expanding horizons of the mind and the spirit.* Lancaster, PA: Technomic, pp. 155–167.

Neugebauer, B. (2000). Creating community, generating hope, connecting future and past: The role of rituals in our lives. *Child Care Information Exchange, 136,* pp. 48–51.

Noddings, N. (1992). *The challenge to care in schools: An alternative approach to education.* New York: Teachers College Press.

Nolde, E. (1934). *Fra Angelico and his times.* (See "empathy"), Retrieved June 5, 2003, from http://www.artlex.com/ArtLex/E.html

Palmer, P. (1998). *The courage to teach: Exploring the inner landscape of a teacher's life.* San Francisco: Jossey-Bass.

Parents Without Partners. (2003). Retrieved September 11, 2003, from www.parentswithoutpartners.org/Support1.htm.

Peters, M. L., Lankshear, C., & Olssen, M. (2003). Introduction. In M. L. Peters, C., C. Lankshear, & M. Olssen, (Eds.), *Critical theory and the human condition.* New York: Peter Lang.

Piaget, J. (1969). *Judgement and the reasoning child.* London: Routledge & Kegan Paul.

Platt, S. (ed). (1993). *Respectfully quoted: A dictionary of quotations.* New York: Barnes & Noble.

Pope, A. (1711). Essay on criticism. In E. F. Kingston (Ed.), *Poems to remember*, Toronto: J. M. Dent & Sons, pp. 188–189.

Powers, S. M., & Barnes, F. M. (2001). Alternative routes for teacher professional development and resources: The MERLOT online community. *NASSP Bulletin, 85*(628), pp. 58–63.

Purkey, S. C., & Smith, M. S. (1983). Effective schools: A review. *Elementary School Journal. 83*, pp. 427–453.

Ravitch, D. (2003). *The language police.* New York: Alfred A. Knopf.

Richardson, J., & Robinson, C. (1987). The Georgia Principals' Institute. *NASSP Bulletin*, 71(495), pp. 20, 22-23.

Roberts, P. (2001). Freedom, justice, and understanding. *Journal of Educational Thought/Revue de la pensée éducatif. 35*(2), pp. 149–156.

Roethlisberger, F. J. (1941). *Management and morale.* Cambridge, MA: Harvard University Press.

Russell, C. L., Bell, A. C., & Fawcett, L. (2000). Navigating the waters of Canadian environmental education. In T. Goldstein & D. Selby (Eds.), *Weaving connections: Educating for peace, social and environmental justice.* Toronto: Sumach, pp. 196–217.

Rutherford, J. E. (1990). A place called home: Identity and the cultural politics of difference. In J. E. Rutherford (Ed.), *Identity: Community, culture, difference.* London: Lawrence Wishart, pp. 12–24.

Senge, P. M. (1990). *The fifth discipline: The art and practice of the learning organization.* New York: Doubleday.

Sergiovanni, T. J. (1992). *Moral Leadership: Getting to the heart of schooling.* San Francisco: Jossey-Bass.

Sergiovanni, T. J. (1993, April). *Organizations or communities? Changing the metaphor changes the Theory.* Paper presented at the annual meeting of the American Education Research Association, Atlanta, Georgia.

Sergiovanni, T. J. (1996). *Leadership for the schoolhouse: How is it different? Why is it important?* 1st ed., San Francisco: Jossey-Bass.

Shavelson, R. J., & Towne, L. (Eds.) (2002). *Scientific research in education: Committee on scientific principles for education research.* In Center for Education. Division of Behavioral and Social Sciences and Education. National Research Council. Washington, DC: National Academy Press. Retrieved August 16, 2003, from http://www.nap.edu/execsumm/ 0309082919.html

Shields, C. M. (2003). *Good intentions are not enough: Transformative leadership for communities of difference.* Lanham, MD: Scarecrow.

Shields, C. M., Edwards, M., & Sayani, A. (Eds.) (2004). *Inspiring practices: Spirituality and educational leadership.* Lancaster, PA: Pro>Activ.

Shields, C. M., & Seltzer, P. A. (1997). Complexities and paradoxes of community: Toward a more useful conceptualization of community. *Educational Administration Quarterly. 33*(4), pp. 413–439.

Sidorkin, A. M. (1997). Carnival and domination: Pedagogies of neither care nor justice. *Educational Theory, 47*(2), pp. 229–239.

Sidorkin, A. M. (1999). *Beyond discourse: Education, the self, and dialogue.* Albany: State University of New York.

Sidorkin, A. M. (2002). *Learning relations.* New York: Peter Lang.

Simon, H. (1945). *Administrative behavior.* New York: Macmillan.

Smith, A. (1976). *An inquiry into the nature and causes of the wealth of nations.* Chicago: University of Chicago Press. (Original work published 1776.)

Starratt, J. R. (1995). *Leaders with vision: The quest for school renewal.* Thousand Oaks, CA: Corwin.

Starratt, R. J. (1991). Building an ethical school: A theory for practice in educational leadership. *Educational Administration Quarterly. 27*(2), pp. 155–202.

Stedmans Online Medical Dictionary. (2003). *Empathy.* Retrieved August 20, 2003, from http://216.251.241.163/semdweb/InternetSOMD/ASP/1513643.asp

Swaim, J. F. (2002). Laughing together in carnival: A tale of two writers. *Language Arts, 79*(4), pp. 337–46.

Swartz, D. (1997). *Culture and power: The sociology of Pierre Bourdieu.* Chicago: University of Chicago Press.

Swingewood, A. (1998). *Cultural theory and the problem of modernity.* New York: St. Martin's.

Taylor, F. W. (1997). Scientific management. In D. S. Pugh (Ed.), *Organization theory.* Toronto: Penguin. pp. 2-3– 222 (Original work published 1912.)

Thayer-Bacon, B. J. (2003). *Relational "(e)pistemologies".* New York, Peter Lang.

Toohey, K., Waterstons, B., & Julé-Lemke, A. (2000). Community of learners, carnival, and participation in a Punjabi Sikh classroom. *The Canadian Modern Language Review, 56*(3), pp. 421–436.

Trapp, J. (1958). Ed., *Martin Buber: To hallow this life. An anthology.* New York: Harper & Brothers.

Tyack, D. B. (1974). *The one best system: A history of American urban education.* Cambridge, MA: Harvard University Press.

Valle, J. W., & Aponte, E. (2002). IDEA and collaboration: A Bakhtinian perspective on parent and professional discourse. *Journal of Learning Disabilities.* 35(5), pp. 469–79.

van Oers, B. (2001). Educational forms of initiation in Mathematical culture. *Educational Studies in Mathematics,* 46(1-3), pp. 59–85.

Vendler, H. (2001). Value: Ups and downs with Harvard during a lifetime of involvement, a senior scholar comes to discern a university community of affection, justice, and reciprocity. *Harvard Magazine, 104*(2), pp. 48–50.

Voltaire, J. F. M. A. de (1759 /1999). *Candide.* D. Gordon (Trans., Ed.), Boston: Bedford/St. Martins.

Vygotsky, L. S. (1978) *Mind in society: The development of higher psychological processes.* Cambridge: Harvard University.

Walmsley & Associates (2003). *Play therapy,* Retrieved August 10, 2003, from http//www.walmsley.ca/play_therapy.htm

Ward, A., & Bouvier, R. (2001). *Resting lightly on Mother Earth.* Calgary, Canada: Detselig.

Weber, M. (1997/1924). Legitimate authority and bureaucracy. In D. S. Pugh (Ed.), *Organization theory: Selected readings.* New York: Penguin. pp. 1–15 (Original work published 1947)

Weeks, J. (1990). The value of difference. In J. E. Rutherford (Ed.), *Identity: Community, culture, difference.* London: Lawrence Wishart, pp. 89–119.

Wheatley, M. (1993). *Leadership and the new science.* San Francisco: Berrett-Koehler.

Young, I. M. (1990). *Justice and the politics of difference.* Princeton, NJ: Princeton University Press.

Zohar, D. (1997). *ReWiring the corporate brain: Using the new science to rethink how we structure and lead organizations.* San Francisco: Berrett-Koehler.

SUBJECT INDEX

Studies in the Postmodern Theory of Education

General Editor
Shirley R. Steinberg

Counterpoints publishes the most compelling and imaginative books being written in education today. Grounded on the theoretical advances in criticalism, feminism, and postmodernism in the last two decades of the twentieth century, Counterpoints engages the meaning of these innovations in various forms of educational expression. Committed to the proposition that theoretical literature should be accessible to a variety of audiences, the series insists that its authors avoid esoteric and jargonistic languages that transform educational scholarship into an elite discourse for the initiated. Scholarly work matters only to the degree it affects consciousness and practice at multiple sites. Counterpoints' editorial policy is based on these principles and the ability of scholars to break new ground, to open new conversations, to go where educators have never gone before.

For additional information about this series or for the submission of manuscripts, please contact:

Shirley R. Steinberg
c/o Peter Lang Publishing, Inc.
29 Broadway, 18th floor
New York, New York 10006

To order other books in this series, please contact our Customer Service Department:

(800) 770-LANG (within the U.S.)
(212) 647-7706 (outside the U.S.)
(212) 647-7707 FAX

Or browse online by series:
www.peterlang.com